Chauvet – The D

Steve I

Under fair use

Copyright © 2013 Steve Meads

Special Edition

In memory of;

Charlie Francis

5th February 1976 - 4th July 2015

Table of Contents

Chapter 1: The Discovery

Chapter 2: The Journey

Chapter 3: The Hand of Man

Chapter 4: "My God, It's full of Stars!"

Chapter 5: The Sphinx of Ra

Chapter 6: Deeper into Egypt

Chapter 7: Ra, the Creative Power

Chapter 8: The Unknown

Chapter 1 The Discovery

On the 21st December 2012, Millions of people around the world were wondering if certain predictions were going to come true. Many others carried on with the full belief that nothing would happen and life would go on as usual. We now find ourselves at the start of a new year and for almost everyone life is going on as normal.

I say almost everyone because, for me, everything changed. I had always suspected that there was more to Human history than we currently know and that the secrets of our past were not known or were being kept hidden in some manner. We've made slow progress towards discovering our ancient roots, but step by step, we are uncovering that which is hidden, or lost. Something had been discovered yet things were still hidden. Hidden in more ways than was, at first, immediately obvious.

It had not long passed mid-day when I decided to browse a popular movie library and I came across a documentary called "Chauvet – *Cave of Forgotten Dreams*". It was the first time I had seen this documentary though it may not have been the first time I had seen the images, it's just that the images had never really opened my eyes before. I sat there amazed as each section of the cave was unveiled to me. Stunned at the level of skill these ancient artists were acquainted with. Fascinated by the way they managed to transfer their world onto a cave wall with, what we believe to be, minimal tools.

Effectively, I was discovering the cave for the first time in its entirety. Little did I suspect that what I was seeing was the start of something incredible! It was the start of a journey that was to lead me through a story that had been, in more ways than one, hidden, yet is now available for everyone.

Let's not forget that these paintings are approximately 30,000 years old. The cave was sealed off around 20,000 years ago from a suggested landslide. Located in the Ardèche department of southern France, the cave was discovered in 1994 and contains hundreds of animal paintings showing at least 13 different species and even some that are very rarely or even never found in any other ice age art. Usually we see cattle and horses in many other cave paintings, but here we see predatory animals too, like lions, hyena and bear. It is relatively easy to distinguish each animal from another. Some of the animals are separate from others whilst the rest are stacked on top of each other in order to show, not only movement, but a herd of the same species.

The rock face has been cleaned before the paintings were applied and in places they have left parts of the original wall in order to help build up the pictures and to blend in with the paintwork. They have even etched the cave wall to create an almost 3D style image of the painted subjects. But we must take note that a lot of other 'etchings' were actually created by bears that inhabited the cave. We can clearly see where the bears have been scratching the walls and where some bears spent their last moments as we see skulls and other bones lying around on the floor of the cave. It's clear that this cave had been used for a very long period of time but some debate the age of the paintings yet the most recent dating (2012) puts them around the [Aurignacian]() period, approximately 30,000–32,000 BP.

The documentary leads you through the caves and begins to show you the art work on the walls. As I was looking at the art, I was getting the impression that something was not quite right with the pictures. Something was there that just seemed too suggestive to me. Yes, I could clearly see the animals but some of them had not been painted as exactly as other similar ones had been, there were what appeared to be errors. Everything made me look twice. It was like watching a movie but having to rewind it in order to spot the mistakes the film makers had made but it also made me feel as though these 'mistakes' had been purposely placed in order to draw you in.

Then, one camera made a close up shot of one particular part of the wall and the image hit me instantly. I immediately recognised it as being something that we may all know, [the eye of Ra]().

It is the feminine counterpart of [Ra](), the Egyptian god of the sun, or the creator, who is often visualised as a falcon. The eye represents Ra's power but is also an independent entity, the eye goddess, mother, sibling, consort, and daughter of the sun god. She is Ra's partner in the grand scheme of things, the life cycle. She is the defender of Ra's reign and she can be rather violent, often represented as a lioness or a snake. She is "[the all seeing eye]()"! This is why this image, and others, have been blended together in such a way that they are hidden yet can be seen.

It was at this point that I believed I may be onto something. I looked at this image and realised that there is another image under, or rather with, the black markings and a deliberate error had been made in order to hide the true intention, yet reveal the other image.

In the next image we see the eye of Ra as we know it. It is the usual symbol we associate with and how it has been portrayed over all these years. Does the above image stretch our current known history back by literally 30,000 years?

There does appear to be some debate over which eye is the real eye of Ra. It may be the left or it may be the right but apparently it doesn't really matter too much. At first, it was the right eye that was connected to Ra and the left was connected to the moon and in one legend Ra had an eye torn out but nobody really knows which one. This tearing out of the eye has been associated with a solar eclipse, where the moon passes in front of the sun. Now I need to break down the first image in order for you to see what is hidden, if you have not already seen it for yourself.

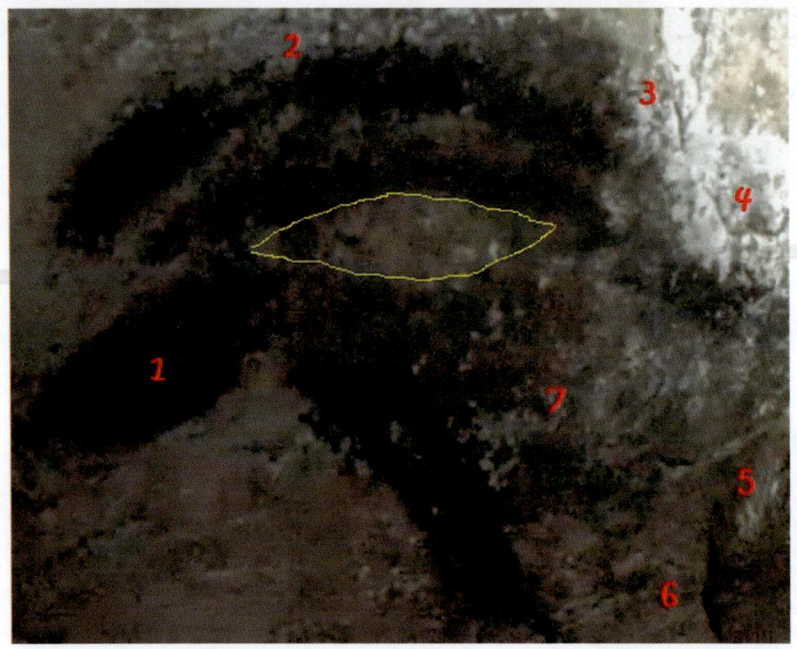

So, number 1 is the eye of the falcon, deliberately painted far to the left so as to not cover up the human eye outlined in yellow. Number 2 is the eyebrow and the grey shading is the forehead. Number 3 is the temple area of the left side of the skull. 4 is the top of the left ear. 5 is the ear lobe. To the right side of the number 6 we see a black line representing the neckline directly below the ear lobe. Number 7 is the top of the cheek below the eye socket. Overall, we have what appears to be the left side of a human face with the eye of Ra painted upon it.

What makes this even more interesting is that this image is supposed to be the head of a horse, but you cannot see the body of the horse at this angle due to it being painted on a less prominent section of the cave wall. This protruding outcrop effectively hides the horse's body when approaching it along the path. Try seeing this from any other angle and it just looks odd, unusual and out of place. The horse's body itself is nowhere near as strongly drawn and defined as this image of the eye is.

The next image is the 'horse' in its entirety, but why does it not resemble a horse as we know one from any other ancient cave painting?

You can just make out its rump. It is so poorly defined that I can only imagine that the emphasis on the 'head' was for a very good reason. This is also the only design of its kind in the cave (that I am aware of) whereas we do see four other horses which are so detailed that we can, in my opinion, make out four different breeds of horse. They are painted high up on a wall and stand out clearly from everything else around them. There are at least three other horses painted around the cave.

All of the images in the cave lead you around in circles. They are trying to say something, but they are using other images in the cave to back up and strengthen the message of the first image. So, as we see this 'horse' above, we see the four horses in the picture below. Please take note of the different breeds and is that a half of a horse shoe on the mane of the horse on the right?

If not, what is it? Every time I see these four horses I can only think of the four horsemen of the apocalypse! Why else would they paint four of them and each one is different, as are the horsemen. Are the horsemen supposed to represent something else, like the four seasons perhaps?

Chapter 2 The Journey

So that was it, I was hooked. I had to know more and had to keep watching the documentary. What I found next led me on one of the most strange but mind opening journeys I've ever been on. We must remember that these images are layered in a way that makes you wonder just how intelligent our ancestors were. Every time I look at one image, I see something else deep within it or just on the surface. Each section of the painting has something in it, yet the entire painting is one complete story in itself. You start in one place and get taken to another position only for that to lead you right back to where you started after a slight detour.

When you look at some of the images that are available from various sources you will most probably just see a flat image of the paintings. It's when you see it as it really is, thanks to different levels and angles of lighting, that you realize how clever the artists were. A lot of the images and their trickery require different directions of light, different distances from which to view and possibly a different level of intelligence with which to understand what the paintings are saying. You will understand what I'm saying here as we progress through 30,000 years of our past.

Here is one section of wall;

It looks rather straight forwards, but don't be fooled! This is far, far more than just pictures of lions and rhinos. In this section alone is a map that points to an area of land, a set of stars that are Cygnus, the well documented 'bird man' and maybe even the artist's self-portrait.

Fasten your seat belts as this journey is going to get a bit bumpy, but I think you're going to enjoy the ride.

My journey began over on the left side of the above image.

One thing stood out that made me wonder if what I was seeing was what I thought it was. I thought I was looking at Egypt and the Nile, or rather the Nile as it would have been 30,000 years ago. I was not prepared to believe that I'd not only found the eye of Ra, but also its Egyptian connection in a cave that had been sealed for so very long.

Here is that section in the next image. Notice the reddish dots in a line to the right and the three black dots near the centre of the picture. Surely the black dots cannot be the Pyramids! Can they? The red dots seemed to be hinting at a direction.

The next portion of the main image to catch my eye was something that resembled a nuclear explosion, or some form of eruption. Were the red dots leading me to this?

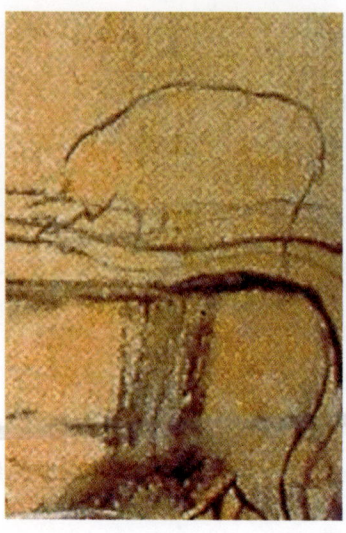

It was as if this odd looking elephant on really long legs that had disguised itself as an explosion was trying to say 'look at me!' So, back I went, back to the start of the wall and I took another look.

I could see the section that I thought might be the Nile and decided to try looking at it as if it really was the Nile. I followed the line to the left until I rounded the head of the lion and noticed an error (or deliberate error).

The lion's eye is above its eyebrow/lash! I made a mental note and carried on down to its slightly open mouth. At this point I opened up an online map and tried to make a comparison.

Going by this map, I was able see how the cave painting fits into this image. The area that I thought was the Nile IS the Nile and the lions head is the West side of Northern Africa.

The eye of the lion is a landmark and the eyelash represents a gradient and/or mountain range. The lion's mouth is a long valley.

The landmark that is the lion's eye could possibly be what is todays [Marakesh](#) (the land of God), and the eyelash is the mountain range below it. Marakesh sprang up sometime in the [Neolithic period](#), but the 'map' may suggest that this was an important area long before that. If so, what lies beneath the ancient city?

11

The lion's mouth is the valley that starts directly above Nouakchott (place of the winds), which also leads us to a rather interesting landmark which is known as the Richat Structure and was formed from a volcano.

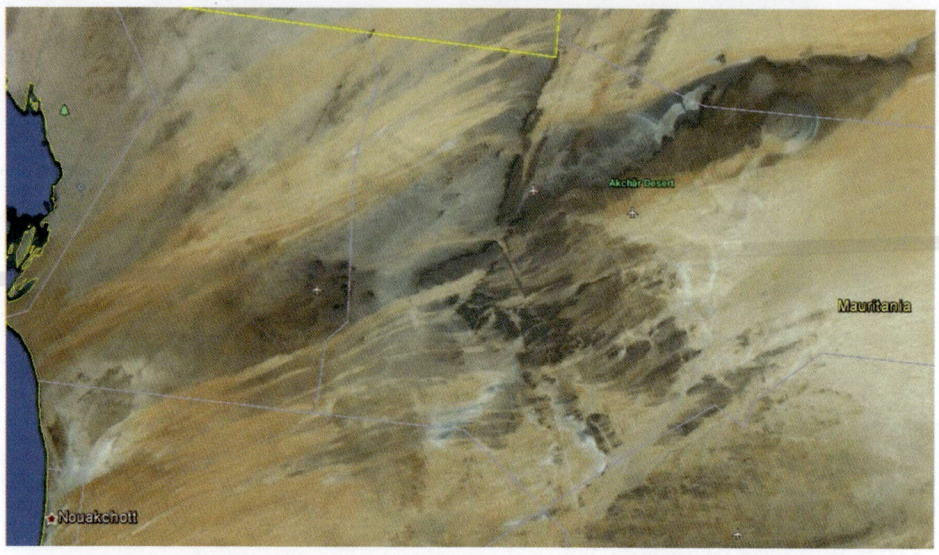

After looking at that I decided to mark the areas out on the cave painting and see what else would pop up. I still have not forgotten about the row of dots on the far right of the map. They're like stepping stones towards the eruption.

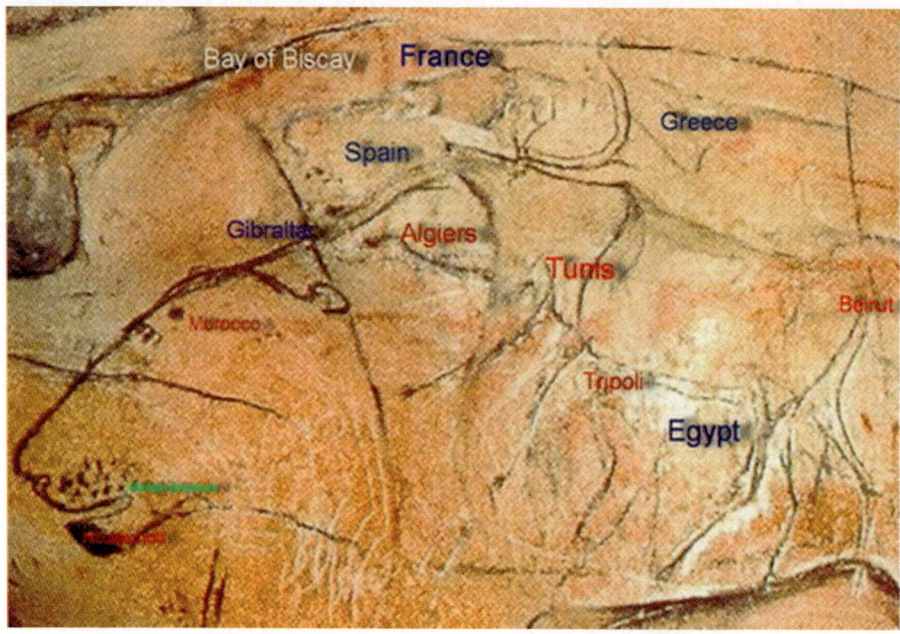

I began looking to the East, towards this unusual marking that was obscured by several long horned rhino. I had to follow the trail that was now gradually opening itself up in front of me. I had several emotions and thoughts running through me that were elating yet disbelieving at the same time. Were these images real? Was this some form of major hoax? Had I really discovered something that has not been truly seen by anyone else for 30,000 years? Could it be that someone else had already found all this and was just not allowed to say anything? Was this part of the ancient secrets that many cults, clubs and secret societies lay claim to? I faced the rising sun….

Going on the basis that I was looking at a map, I wondered if any of the scribbling's on the wall were in any way related to the terrain as I had already begun to discover. By focusing on the area I was interested in, I noticed two marks. Number 1 has two faint lines above it whilst number 2 has a slightly cone shaped line above it. I opened up a map and began estimating where this region would be, if it existed.

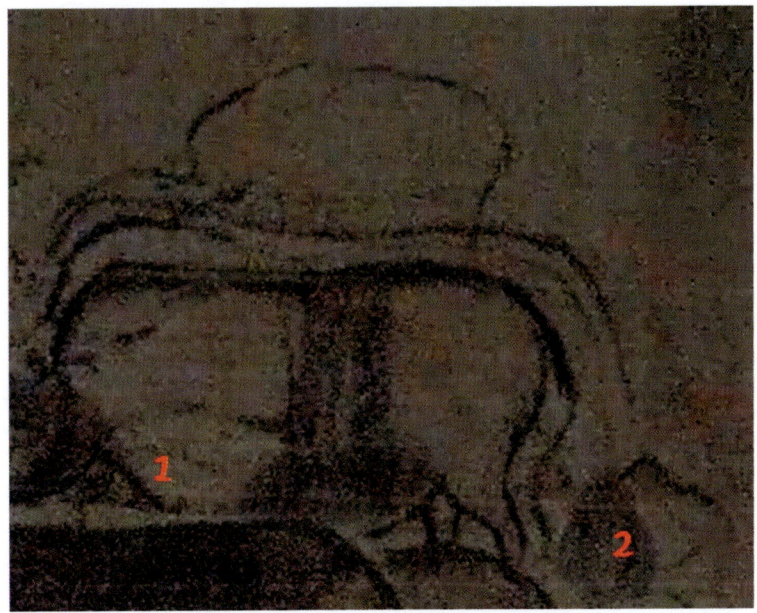

I was not to be disappointed. I found myself in a region below Tehran at an area called Namak Lake and sat right next to it was something that just blew me away and confirmed the eye of Ra painting, the map and the image of an explosion from the cave. 1 and 2 are the mountainous ranges marked on the cave map. In dead centre is the eye of Ra, in this case a crater. But there is so much more to this region than first meets the eye as you will shortly see.

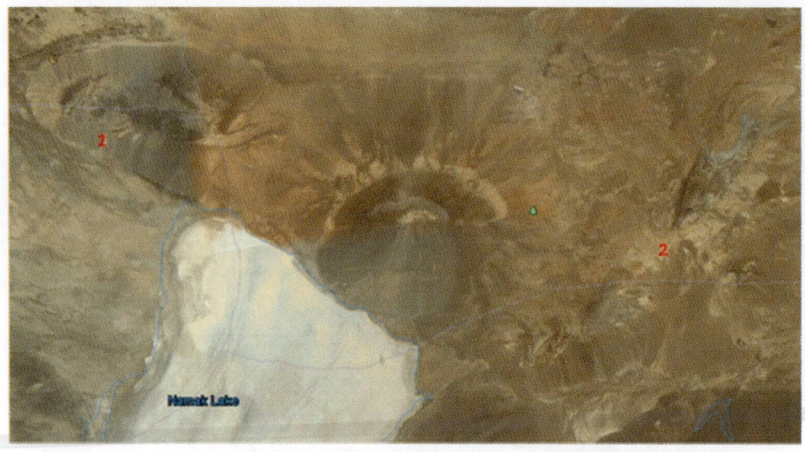

Here is a closer look at the crater and you should be able to see how very similar it is to the eye of Ra with its 'tear drop' design;

The funny thing is that the painting of the eye and the explosion both resemble this one crater. Remember me saying that all the images were layered and that they back each other up in some manner. Well, here is the first bit of evidence for that. I'll add a side by side image to compare;

Notice how in this comparison below that the falcons eye that was moved to the left also matches the darker oval patch to the lower left of the crater. I can only imagine the reason for moving the dark line below the eye. It was to preserve the image of the face in the cave.

This design below the eyes that resembles a pointed, but not fully formed, letter K can also be found on the cave painting near the explosion, it's just that it has been moved away from the explosion in order to distract from the truth.

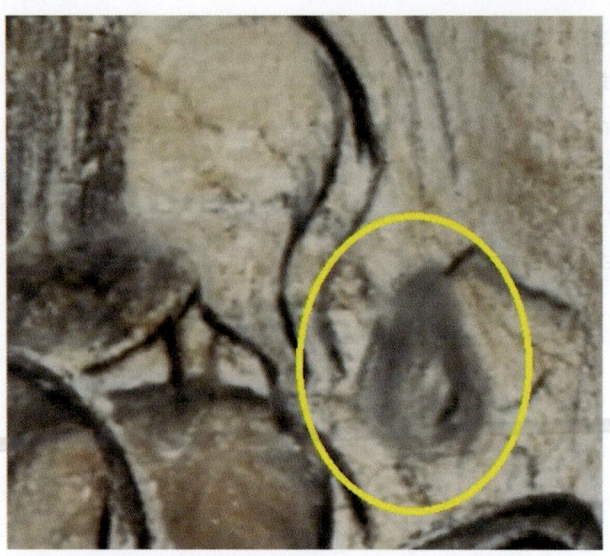

I am becoming more and more convinced that to understand the entirety of these paintings, you have to have reached a certain level of knowledge about the planet that we all live on. We know about the eye of Ra, so it could be spotted. We know about the geography of our planet, so we can see the things upon it from great distances. You will see more of this as the caves unfold and the dream is unlocked. There are more things that we are able to compare to the world we now know today by studying our past and looking to the future.

We're going to stay in this area for a moment as there are some things that we need to take a look at and think about before we move back into the cave.

Firstly, how did these people from so long ago know about this crater? How did the 'tear drop' design of Ra end up on the ground beneath the crater? Was it man made? These questions will be raised even further as we look at the area in more detail.

If we zoom into the patch directly below the crater and to the left of the tear drop, we see an odd image. Is it a bird or does it more resemble a plesiosaur or is it just a natural occurrence that just happens to look like something else? Well, before you decide, let's go over everything else first as well.

Here we see the 'bird' below the crater

Yes, it does look very much like some form of creature, but don't forget that this image can be seen from 130Km above the ground and that the outline of this beast is made entirely of mountains!! But as we move on, things just get weirder especially when you use a map and zoom out and look at a wider area you see other unusual things like this snake (remember the feminine side of Ra being a snake or a lioness?)

Its head is to the right, whilst its body slithers its way across to the top left corner of the picture. The next image is a close up of its head showing its two nostrils,

Complete with forked tongue!!

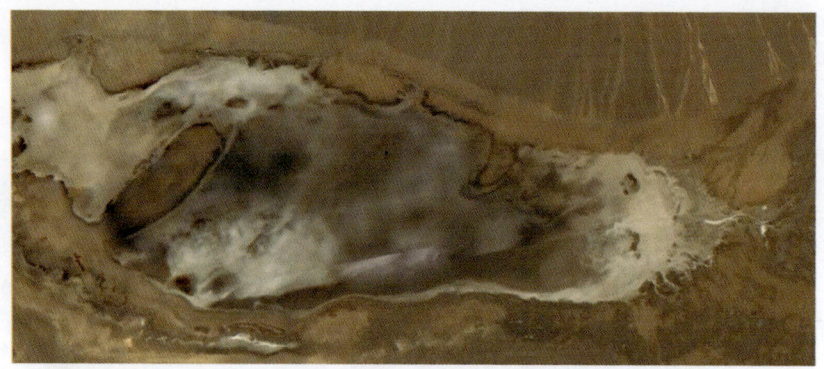

So we have now come some way to partly confirm the origin of the legend about the feminine Ra, all we need now is a lioness. Luckily, someone made one for us a while back. Looking North East of the snakes head we find this, a lioness, hunting, with its tail in the air, which you can easily make out from 430kms above the Earth

Just how did they have knowledge of these images on the ground? What made these people combine them into a legend that would last for so very long? How did we forget these connections?

Is [Erich von Däniken](#) correct in his theory that we were visited by space travelling peoples many thousands of years ago? When you've read his book "[*Chariots of the Gods*](#)" the idea does not seem so far-fetched when you compare this to what we are finding. Especially once you've read many of the stories and legends of the ancient gods like Ra, for example, and how they came here from above to 'create' and also as to how some of them decided to leave! Or was there a strong spiritual force at work?

We've got just one more place to visit from this general area before going back to the caves, Göbekli Tepe. The reason for this stop over is 1, its location and 2, a carved rock. We will visit this place again later but that's for another item in the paintings.

Göbekli Tepe is located in the South-eastern Anatolia Region of Turkey and is a Neolithic site perched on top of a mountain. It is believed to be the oldest religious temple site and is now under continual study.

The carved rock in question is this one;

I find it way too much of a coincidence that it just so happens to resemble the cave painting of the explosion and that this rock just so happens to have a lion carved on it that has almost the exact same stance as the lion we see North-East of the snake and crater.

This feline with its front paws and tail in the air is not just found in these two places. Further research led me to discover that it is also found on a cave wall in Seminole park, Texas, USA.

You also have to wonder how this particular style has been kept alive for so long seeing as we still use this pose in modern heraldry. In this next image we see a lion in this pose on the Temple of Kom Ombo. The Temple is different from many others as it is a double temple built during the Ptolemaic dynasty in the Egyptian town of Kom Ombo and has evidence of Roman interference at some point.

What does this posing feline have to say to us? Why has it become an image that has stood the test of time?

We cannot underestimate the skill and required knowledge of the cave artists. We assume their tools and other equipment were simple and perhaps they really were, but that is all you need when you have the knowledge and ability to create a work of art! Did [Michelangelo](#) use a high-tech paint spraying gun when he painted the [Sistine chapel](#)? No, he used simple and basic brushes, yet he managed to paint the subjects in such a way that it astounds everyone who sees it. His ability to envisage the end result and apply techniques to such architecture is rather incredible and we must, or at least try, to give the same recognition to the Chauvet painters.

Why? Well, they not only layered the paintings and hid items of importance in them, but they also carefully selected each portion of the cave wall to help them represent the real world items they were trying to recreate and point towards.

When we see the region of the crater and the salt lake right next to it, we see a distinct curved line separating the two. We also see the same curved line separating the map of Egypt/Africa from the area that contains the rhino and the explosion. In the caves, this curved line is the cave wall itself and not something created by the artists.

You can see how the effect of lighting and viewing the cave wall at the correct angles can show us exactly what was being shown. When you think about it a bit deeper, just how lucky were the artists to be able to find a portion of wall that had a very similar curve to the lake area! Or is it just another coincidence?

I have not forgotten the three black dots near the Nile that I previously mentioned, but they connect to another portion of this wall's paintings that we have not reached yet and I will be covering those a bit later. For now, we're going to go back to the main section and look at the middle portion where the hand of man takes a more obvious role.

Chapter 3 The Hand of Man

In the documentary we are shown a few sections where man has definitely left his mark. One section is made up purely of a hand where the artist has left prints all over the wall. The hand prints are the stereo-typical image that we have come to know about cave art and it's one of the definers that makes us, us. The "I was here" statement is loud and clear!

It's also mentioned that there are no full human figures in the cave and that the only other representation of humans is a rather erotic image that can only be seen from a particular angle. This, below, is the image they are describing;

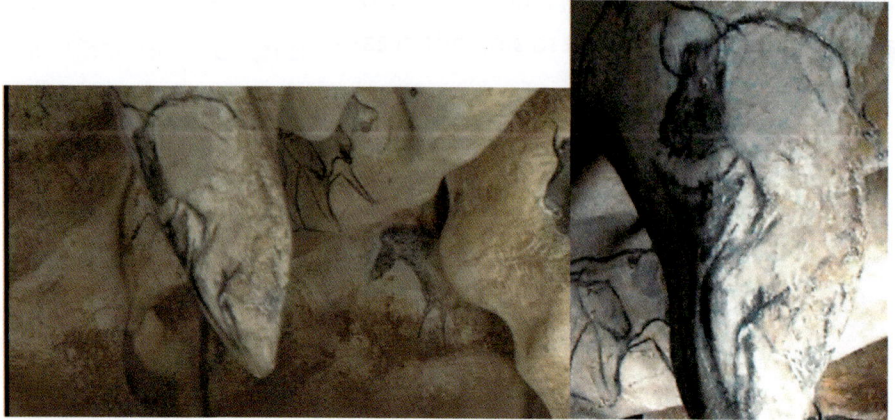

It is declared to be "the only partial representation of a human in the entire cave". Well, I'm sorry, and I mean no disrespect, but they're wrong. There are actually several other representations of humans. Some are sexual in content and are a combination of both art work and the natural stone formations where the artist's eye has recognized a shape. Some seem to be the actions of man, what we do and how we do it.

Right back at the start of the paintings there is a face on the wall.

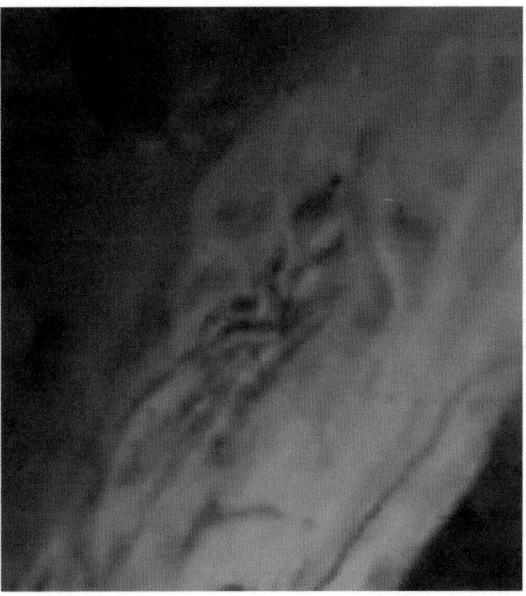

That face even seems to be connected to an upper torso that may possibly be wearing items of clothing. Is he waving with his left hand held up above his left eye?

As we move further in we come to the 'horse' that is the eye of Ra, just around the corner you can see what appears to be the outline of a full human figure. But this figure has been played with. The artist has toyed with us. It has been drawn in a way that mimics the Sistine chapel's artwork. You have to see it from a very tight angle in order to complete the picture; otherwise the figure becomes lost, as you will see

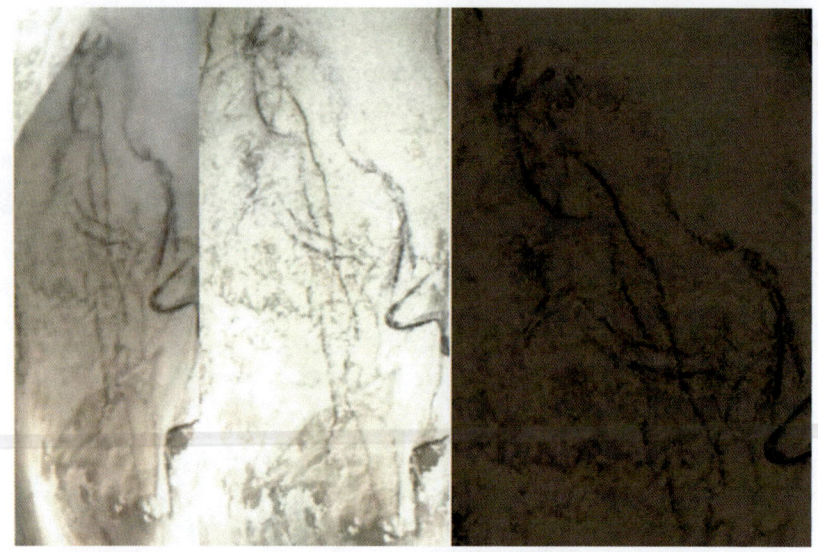

On the left, we can see how this appears to be a human. There is a head connected to a neck and left shoulder and part of the left arm. We can work out the lower left leg, the thigh of the right leg and possibly something being held over the right shoulder. But as we move around to a more 'full-on' look at the image it stretches and distorts and becomes less visible. The head no longer appears to be connected to the neck, the lower half has almost disappeared and so it becomes less human. In the third pic, we can barely make it out to be anything but a few curved lines drawn randomly around a crack in the rock. This is another example of being in the right place to 'see'.

Walking through the cave again and we see more images of man. There is one that looks like a hand holding and preparing to throw a spear. This 'spear' also forms part of another message within the art and we'll be getting to that part later. This is one of those 'remember what I said earlier' about how we have to keep going over the images, backwards and forwards throughout the cave in order to clarify and verify each picture with other bits and to build the complete story.

The next image is that of the feathered end of a spear whilst a right hand grabs it. You can see the fore-arm too and what may be a bracelet on the wrist. This is just one of mans 'activities' as we were, and still are, rather busy. It does strike me odd as to why they have hardly represented themselves. You'd think they would want to show what they were and how they lived, but instead, we see them hiding away as though they are not the most special beings on Earth. Perhaps, that is the point!

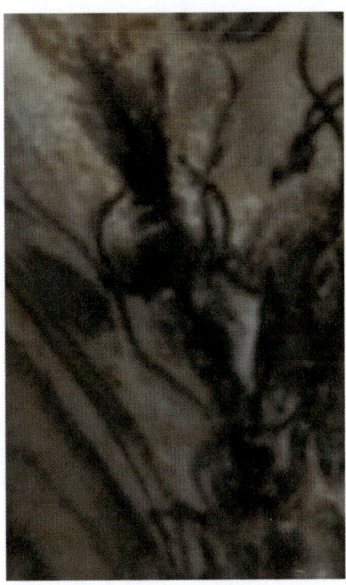

Next to the spear we have a typical Neolithic representation of a female. Added is a sculpture to show the comparison. This female is also a 'double image'. It contains two items that will be discussed later on. The spear may possibly be connected too, depending on interpretation.

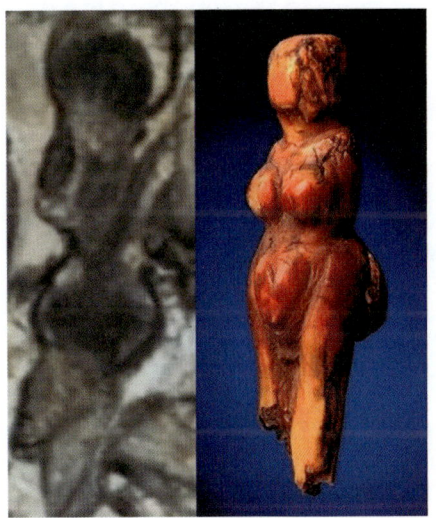

With the woman and the man holding the spear in the same picture together we can see what could be read as though the female was supporting the male by 'cheering him on' as he dresses in the skin of a buffalo or cow/bull, possibly holding a shield in his left and the spear in his right.

It tends to support the idea that we really did used to wear the skins of our kills in order to get closer to the prey we were hunting.

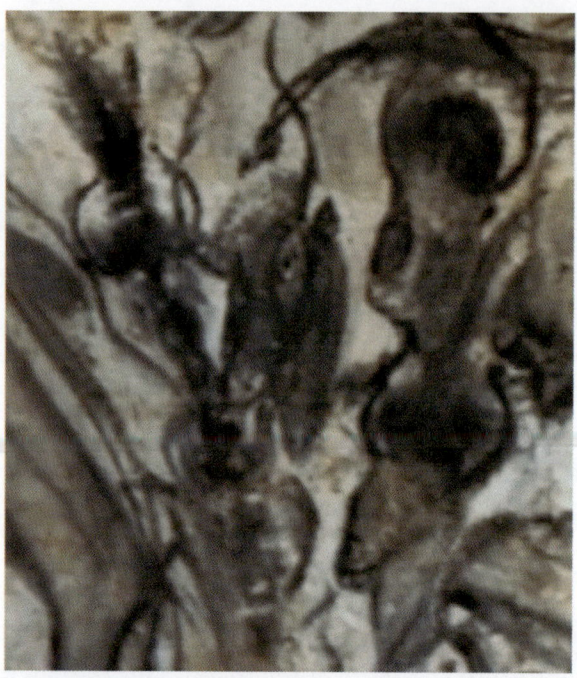

In the next one we can see two legs as though it is a person in the action of swimming. We see his feet near the top right corner, left leg is bent towards the centre and moving more to the left there is a dark patch that could be the head breaking the water line. Also note the 'ripple' effect just above the feet.

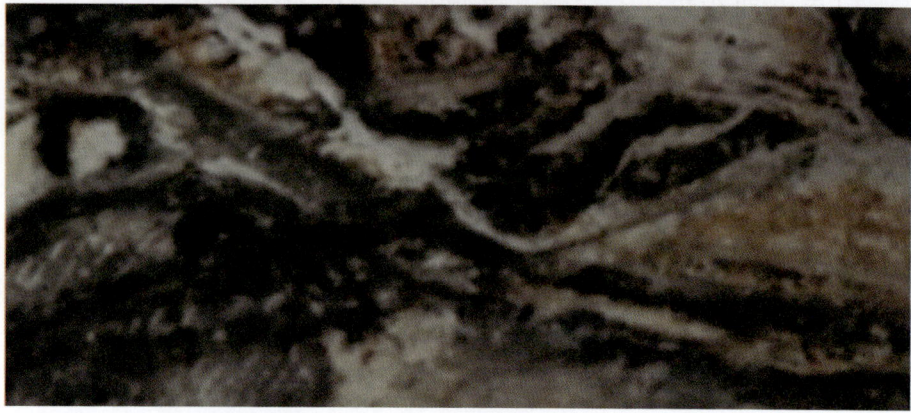

In the centre of the main painting there is a V shaped cavity in the wall that is adorned with the female lower half. This portion of the wall uses the wall itself and the art work to suggest quite a bit about the female form. There even appears to be a few phallic symbols in there too, but they have been cleverly crafted out of the natural surface of the rock unless a very pale paint texture was used. I will leave it to you to work out the representations here.

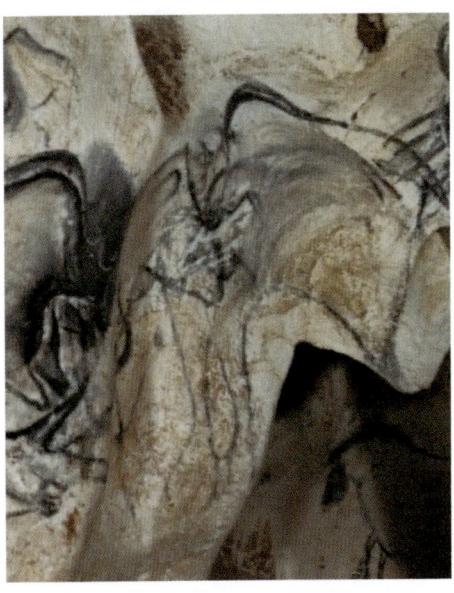

On the main wall, we see several rhino in various places. A couple of them have been placed in a position to hint at what the artist saw in the pattern of the cave wall. The rhino's horns are placed in a suggestive manner

The rhino above made me laugh as its ears look more like human eyes. The rhino appears to have a cheeky grin on its face. You can almost imagine the artist sitting there with a big smile on his face as he painted away, knowing that someone would see it someday and understand the intent of the horns position. Here are the rhino's ears up close

This next face is rather awkward to see. It's one of those things that may take a while to actually spot, but once you've found it; you won't be able to stop seeing it. It also requires a quick return to Göbekli Tepe in order to assist you with what the face actually looks like. This face in the cave is blended in with a set of lions and appears to be part of a collar that a lion is wearing.

Here is the main image of the set with the lion in question in the lower right corner. You can also see the 'swimmer' from earlier. The face is below the swimmer on the part that would be the lion's neck just behind its jaw.

Now, we'll zoom into the area in question and, hopefully, you'll see it right away. It stood out rather well for me. Here, are two versions;

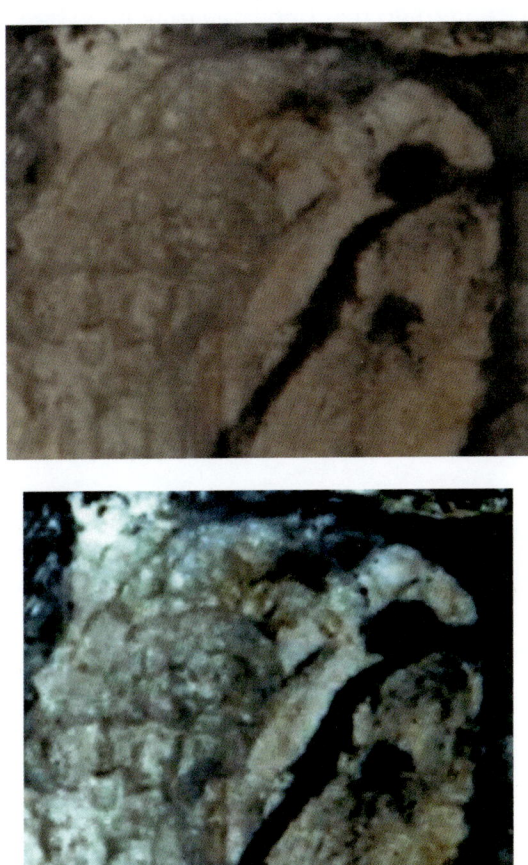

The face is now in the lower left corner with a statue from Göbekli Tepe to help give an idea as to how the face appears;

The face also appears to be wearing some form of headgear. It has a beard and a moustache that seems rather refined and well looked after. If these paintings are anything to go by, then they may have had a culture far more advanced than what we currently think of. Cave dwelling hunters that had the time and inclination to take care of their appearance?

There is one other face that I have found, but I am saving that one for a bit later for another portion of the walls story.

Chapter 4 "My God, It's full of Stars!"

Moving from the central images of the wall, we now head to our right and come across a rather odd selection of things that, at first, didn't make much sense. You see a horned cow or bull of some description, the spear, the buffalo or cow/bull, the woman cheering the hunter on and a mixture of other things, including something that has an extremely long nose and crab-like claws for feet (we'll get to him later), but there was something else. Near the top you see a hippo like creature with its mouth open and a waggling tongue. I bypassed that the first time round thinking it was so odd and unusual, but ended up coming back to it and making one of the most stunning finds. Here is the section in question;

I just couldn't get that strange hippo out of my mind. It is the only animal portrayed in such a way. The image looks unfinished as there is a curved line above the hippo that has been carved into the rock rather than painted. I then saw it had no legs, but there *was* a symbol very similar to the make-up of the woman below the hippo. It was at this point that I had worked it out!

It's a star, or rather the representation of one, specifically, the way the ancient Egyptians represented them. This was a mind blower! Here we see the

Goddess [Hathor-Sekhmet](#) with the solar (star) disc on her head held in place by two lunar horns, next to it is one of the 'stars' from the picture above;

We can see three stars in a vertical line below the hippo in the main image, but the bull over on the left has one too. The hand holding the spear also seems to form part of another star. The outer line of the hand is the second lunar horn. It might also be possible that we have two more stars lower down the length of the spear. I got that far with it, but the hippo was still annoying me. Just why was it so out of place? I decided to broaden my thoughts a little and go with the Egyptian theme that kept popping its head up out of these paintings. I searched for ancient Egyptian star charts and found this;

My jaw hit the floor! There it was, the hippo, but in this image it appears to be more of a lion than a hippo. But I had found it. The open mouth displaying the tongue was the item that gave me positive proof that I really had stumbled upon a message hidden in the entire cave paintings of Chauvet. Looking at this even more and we can see that the curved line above the hippo is actually the back of the alligator climbing the lions back. The curved section that the lion is holding (and a falcon headed man is standing on) is seen next to the hippo. The spear is the same line that the bull is standing on in this Egyptian image. They are the same representation carried from 30,000 years ago through to the ancient Egyptians. The only difference being that the cave painting has been turned on its end to hide the true meaning. Another double message; hidden by simple art.

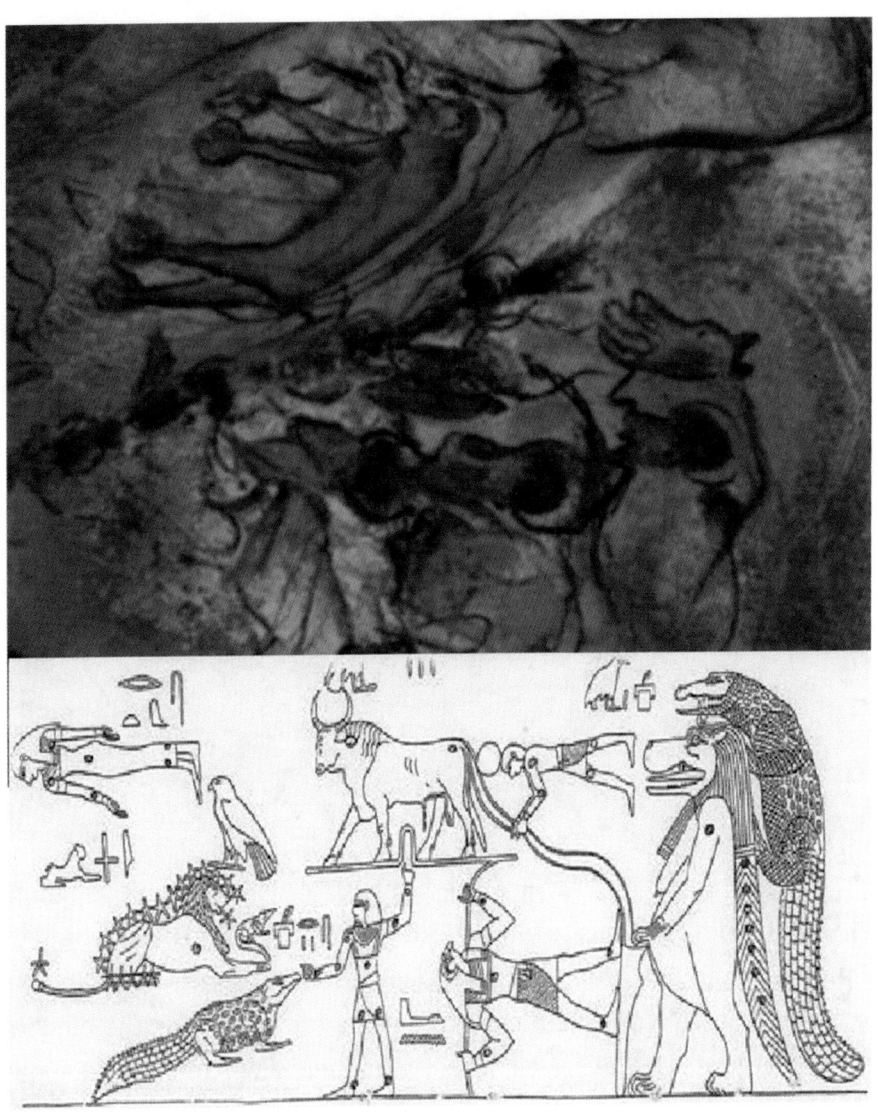

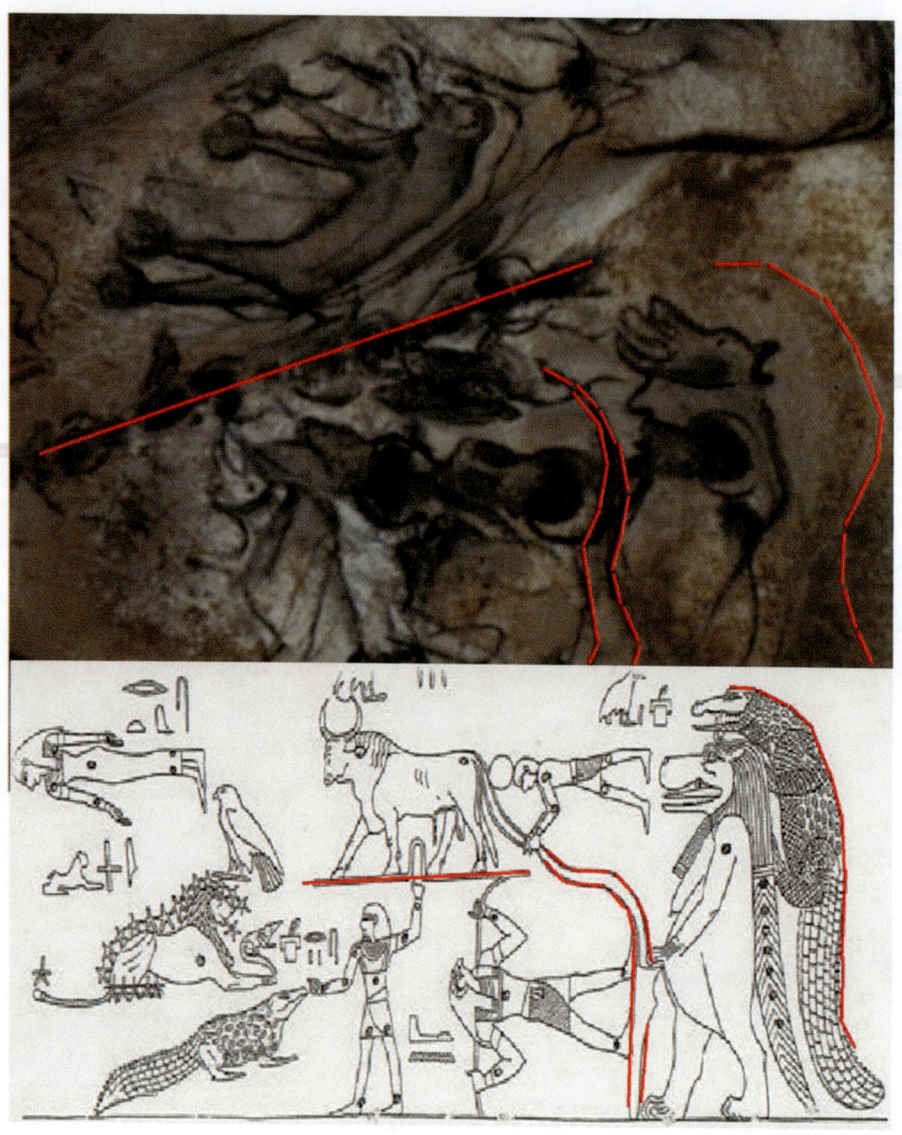

According to the site where I found that image, "The arrangement of the ancient Egyptian northern constellations on the astronomical ceiling of Hall K of the tomb of Seti I. No written record survives for identifying the constellations depicted." (Died 1279BC) Well, now we do have a written record, a painted one. I believe it is Cygnus.

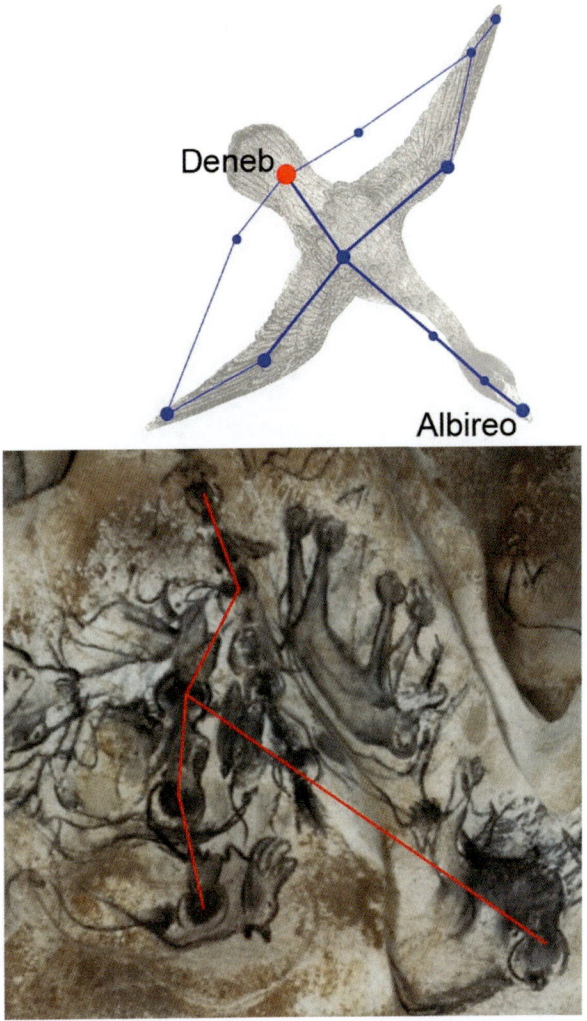

In the painting, Deneb is missing and one wing tip is slightly more forwards than it should be, but it's so very close. If it is not Cygnus, then what else could it be? We have to remember that Cygnus (a bird) was one of the most ancient types of gods.

The theme of a bird god, or bird-man (which I mentioned right at the start of all this), runs throughout history and has links across the globe. Ra was a 'bird-man'. The odd looking creature with the long nose and crab like claws in the painting is a bird-man. We see similar shaped bird-man images elsewhere, like Assyria, Easter Island and the Aztecs

Presented next is a picture of the bird-man from Easter Island and one from Göbekli Tepe next to the bird-man from the cave;

So we begin to see how far the idea of a bird-man went and that it is a repeated them across the globe. All of these stem from the constellation that is Cygnus, otherwise known as the Northern Cross. This cross is another symbol that appears regularly throughout other cave paintings such as the ones at Lascaux where we also see the bird-man;

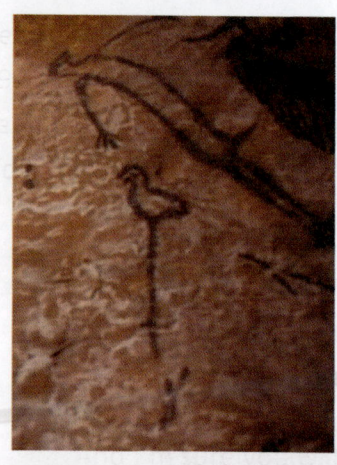

Interestingly, in the Lascaux picture, we can also see a bird on top of a long stick. This is also seen in Egyptian art. Thoth holds such a stick with a bird adorned upon it;

It was believed that Thoth was the leader of the bird-man hybrids whom lived along the Nile many thousands of years ago. The stick which he holds must never touch the ground and in all the pictures we see of this stick from Egypt, none of them do.

Previously, I've mentioned that all the images are backed up and supported by something else in the painting, whether it is a similar image or a link in the story line. Well, we have to go back to the beginning and grab those three black dots that are located next to, what could be the ancient branch of the Nile. When I first saw them I wondered if it were possible that they were the Pyramids, but no, that could not be possible according to our current knowledge of them. But now I had found these three stars below the hippo, the three on the Nile made more sense. Please also take note of the cross that is painted between two of the Niles 'legs'. I wonder how accurate that is to true North.

The Great Pyramid is built on the exact centre of the Earths land mass, in other words its East to West axis corresponds to the longest land parallel across the planet. All three of the Pyramids are also aligned to the three stars that make up Orion's belt. So where do our three Cygnus stars fit in that we can see on the map above?

It turns out that the three main stars that make up the birds body do line up with the Pyramids. Whereas Orion slots into place directly above the Pyramids, as though to mirror each other, Cygnus lines up with the very top of the Pyramids as they begin to set towards the horizon.

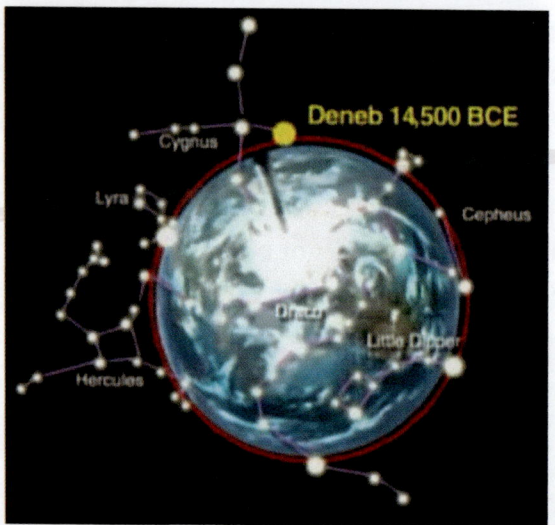

In the age of the Pyramids, Deneb sets itself down on the apex of the second Pyramid each night when you are looking from the direction of Gebel Gibli. So what's with this extra river extending out from the Nile? There is an idea that the Nile has moved many miles away from its original location, which was at the feet of the Pyramids. Personally, I don't think it moved. I'm more inclined to think that this ancient section of the Nile dried up or was redirected. From the documentary The Pyramid Code They provide an example of this old route of the Nile. When you sit the cave map next to the upper region you can see how each one fits in. It is, yet again, another incredible coincidence;

The cave map is not showing the full length of the Nile, it is only showing the upper area, but the map from the documentary does not show that area so well, yet you can still make out the 'elbows' where the Nile bends in the upper region. It is the section above Faiyum Oasis. We also must remember how the cave artists did not always paint things as exactly as we would draw a map these days. I think this is clearly obvious throughout the rest of the cave, but here we see the three black dots on the wrong side of the ancient river as you can see the old river bed above the Pyramids;

I was later to discover just how important this hippo is to the ancient Egyptians. Further study provided me with multiple images of the same creature, both painted and carved. The Pharoah Menes was even killed by one. Menes is credited with the unification of Egypt and, according to legend, related by the priests of the crocodile-god Sobek at Crocodilopolis, Menes had to escape an attack upon himself by his hunting dogs. Apparently he managed to get onto the back of a crocodile which crossed a river taking him to safety.

This is rather interesting when we look at the picture of the crocodile which appears to be on the back of the hippo.. Is this where the legend of Menes' escape comes from? Has the story been muddied over time?

So, here we see further examples of this same hippo with his mouth open, teeth showing and tongue waggling. The Chauvet version is included in the lower left.

Updated edit

In this particular piece of art that shows the hippo, I noticed a line that resembled a spear that was being held by a hand. Here we see a close up of the end of the 'spear' being held by said 'hand'

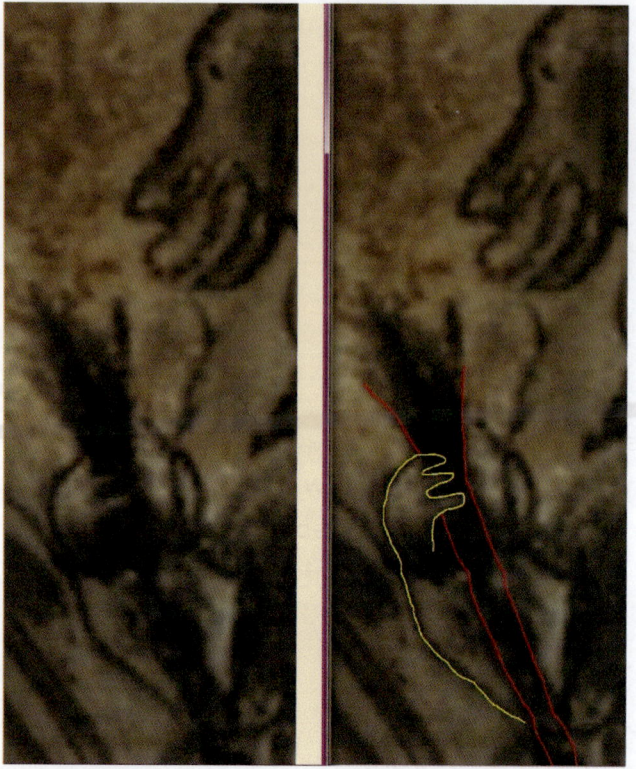

A TV programme that was discussing the spear prompted me to make the connection. The spear is said to have been the one that pierced the body of Christ whilst he was on the cross to see if he was dead.

Looking further into the Egyptian version of this hippo/spear image, I began to notice that it bears a very strong resemblance to a spear being thrusted towards an animal.

And then I found a discussion that Graham Hancock was having which involves several people trying to decide exactly how Cygnus fits into this picture.

He wrote;

"The depictions below show the spatial relation between Dwn-nwy, the Thigh (the Plough) and the Hippopotamus (Draco) (image 1). It is very clear that Dwn-nwy is not behind the hippopotamus, unlike 'mace man' who is clearly behind the hippopotamus on the round Dendera Zodiac (image 2). We all agree that 'Mace man' roughly fits the spatial position of Cygnus, which is behind Draco (image 3). Common sense and astronomical fact brings us to the inevitable conclusion that Dwn-nwy cannot be 'mace man'. And so if 'mace man' is equated to Cygnus, then it follows that Dwn-nwy cannot be Cygnus."

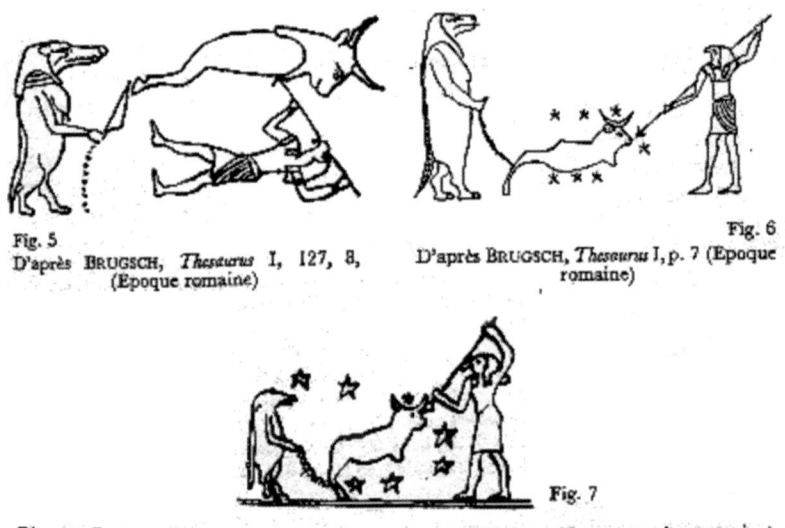

Fig. 5
D'après BRUGSCH, Thesaurus I, 127, 8, (Epoque romaine)

Fig. 6
D'après BRUGSCH, Thesaurus I, p. 7 (Epoque romaine)

D'après ZINNER, Gesch. der Sternkunde – Descr. de l'Egypte (Epoque gréco-romaine)

Fig. 7

I find this all very fascinating as my version of the representation of Cygnus from the cave art covers a far greater area and seems to encapsulate several of these creatures.

looking at it now, it feels like a 'rough-cut' of what is there. Previously I had a few tiny doubts about this bit, but now am a lot more comfortable with it considering the rest of things that I've just pieced together.

So, the question is, is the spear in the art the REAL spear of destiny? Is this the spear that pierced Christs body (the animal in the Egyptian images) whilst Christ was on the cross (Cygnus). Is that the clue to unlocking how to decipher which particular image, or images, relate to Cygnus? Could there be a physical spear in existence that is as described, an all powerful item? Or is it simply yet another misinterpreted story relating to the ancient Egyptian stories of the stars... or in this case, one that originates from cave art that is over 30,000 years old?

Chapter 5 The Sphinx of Ra

Throughout the cave and ancient Egypt, the lioness has a recurring presence. One section of the cave wall, the furthest right of the main image, shows many female lions. None of them show the characteristic of a male, its mane. This does not mean they are all female, as young male lions do not grow a mane until they're older. I think it is safe to say that the majority of them may very well be female. Each lion appears to be entering the environment from one direction. They are all facing the same way, towards the centre section of the painting. There are at least 10 lions in this section.

In other areas of the cave, we do see more images of lions. Two lions appear to be growling at something. It also seems as though the artist has added some markings around the mouth of the uppermost lion in order to give the impression that sound is being made.

Then, in yet another area, we find a few more lions, but this one in particular has a rather different pattern to it. These two lions are poorly drawn and have a slight resemblance to bears, but due to what else appears in this image, lions are our best bet here. Have a good look at the lion in the centre of the image. Shoulder, head, ears, nose and mouth but no eye…

But it does have an eye, two in fact, as there is another feline image painted into the head of this lion. Its ears are the eyes of the other. What would be the eye of the main lion is in fact the nose and mouth of the hidden feline. You can also see some very faint white and grey strokes representing the whiskers of this feline. Here is a close up of this hidden cat;

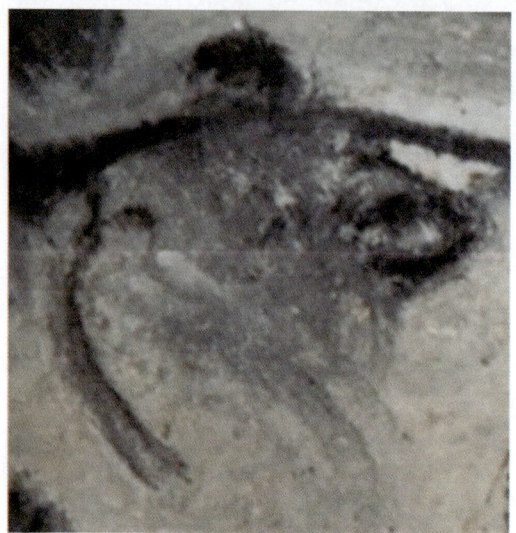

Could it be possible that this is the true face of the Sphinx which is sat next to the Pyramids? Or is there yet another face to be discovered that would have given the ancient Egyptians far more of a reason to re-carve the head of the Sphinx?

If there was a 'more powerful' image sat on the shoulders of the Sphinx, and you hadn't made it, would it not be a good idea to re-carve it in your own likeness in order to demonstrate your power and control? I am more inclined to believe that the sphinx is as old as Dr. R. Schoch has suggested. The weathering on the Sphinx is unmistakeable from the evidence provided.

Ra was represented in a variety of forms one of which was a lion. The Great Sphinx of Giza has the body of a lion whilst its head is most definitely human. Perhaps it was a human head, or at least human-like, prior to its re-carving. So could there really be an image out there somewhere that may have represented the face of Ra on the shoulders of the sphinx? Could it be that this face is in the mix of the cave paintings?

Let's have a look, shall we? We need to look at the very far right side of the section with the 10 lions so that we are left with only a few. Then, you should be able to notice a face, with only 1 eye, its left eye (Ra was said to have lost an eye, but nobody was sure which one), there are two nostrils and a down-turned mouth with, what could be, a pointed beard on its chin. This face may also be wearing a head dress, with a beaded head band to hold it in place. There is the hint of a left ear.

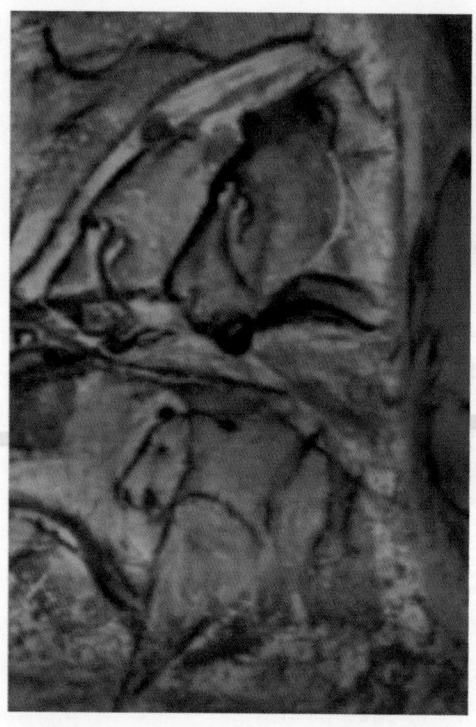

One fascinating thing about the eye is that it is very narrow. The closest way to describe it is of Asian origin, yet it still seems far too narrow for that even. The eye itself is set way into the area closest to what would be the nose. It looks out at you, staring deep into you as though it has some hidden knowledge and authority. Is this the face of Ra? Was this face, complete with head dress, the original head of the Sphinx?

Had anyone taken control of the Egyptian civilisation and wanted to be remembered for all time and maybe even make sure that the old ways were forgotten so that new ideas and practices were followed, you would be sure to do your best to erase the past. Cutting out your own little niche in the corner of an empire would be one sure way of achieving your goals. The decision to re-cut the head may have been hard for some to swallow, but for the controller that was in power at the time, it was an easy choice. Out with the old and in with the new, never to be forgotten.

Below is an edit of the face to try to highlight it in a way that makes it easier to see.

Could the black line that would be the right eye (highlighted with a fine purple line) be telling us that it was the right eye that was ripped out? Is the yellow line the head band, the red circles beads or jewels? Are the white lines the outer edges and folds of some form of head dress?

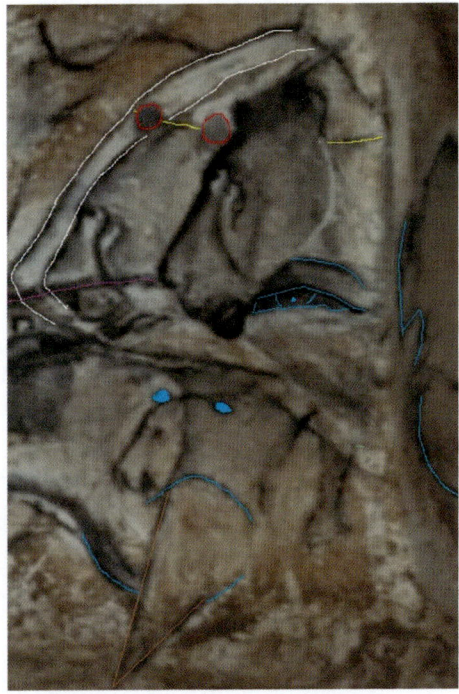

We have to take note of the eye and the beard in particular. We know from many pictures, sculptures and other Egyptian artefacts that those in a position of 'high standing' would paint a black line around their eyes, the men would grow a beard on their chins and the women would have a false beard attached to their chins as we see in this image below;

Was the real reason for these adornments nothing more than wanting to mimic Ra, to become the God that everyone knew of, followed and feared! To be the same as the one who gave you everything! After Adam and Eve ate from the tree, did God not say "they have become like us"!

Could this have been the words of Ra instead?

Or, could it possibly be that this man, Ra, was really from somewhere else and that we not only see his face here, but the ship that he came and left in? Does this add to the "Chariots of the Gods" idea?

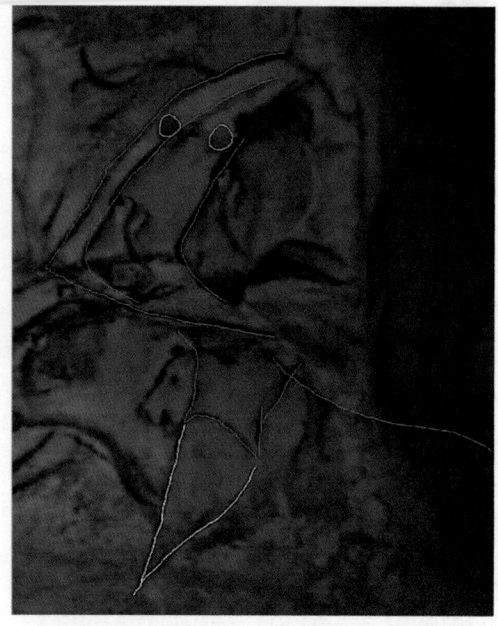

The red lines being the hull, the two circles are portholes and the yellow is the engine of the craft. It's an idea, it may be completely 'way out there', but some other people's ideas have been just as strange so why not this one. How else would anyone have been able to see the markings on the terrain around the crater near Tehran? Could it be at all possible that some of these markings were added or 'created' by Ra's 'power'?

Have the Chauvet paintings revealed everything yet?

Maybe, maybe not, but I decided to take the image of the face one step further and mirrored it. This mirror effect simply repeats the same half giving a full face version. The result was rather stunning and has left me with this question, is it human?

It was at this point that I decided to share this particular image on a popular website and a friend commented as to how remarkably similar it was to an image he was aware of. He posted the image he mentioned and proceeded to tell me who, and how, created it.

This image is also a mirrored image. The original half was created by Leonardo da Vinci and this face is known as the first testament God, Javeh. I can see at least 12 similarities.

Update edit

Looking further into the comparisons between these two faces reveals some very amazing results.

Leonardo di ser Piero da Vinci (15 April 1452 – 2 May 1519) is one of those people that have been blessed enough to be able to leave a long lasting impression on all of mankind. There is so much information about him available worldwide that going into his life here will be too much and wont focus on the point in hand.

Between 1476 to 1478 there is a "gap" in his life. What happened to him? Where did he go and what was it that he saw, or learnt, that drove him to become the master of art, design, invention and hidden messages?

Found among Leonardo's papers are a few personal anecdotes written just after his two year 'gap'. In one account, he details finding a vast and mysterious cave, saying that he felt terrified by the darkness and what might be within. Also, he felt a desire to understand what was inside.

Did this cave contain art that is comparable to the art found in the Chauvet cave

Did he learn his methods, and more, from the study of this art?

In these images we see two faces of very similar appearance. One from Chauvet, the other is from da Vinci's 'Madonna and child'.

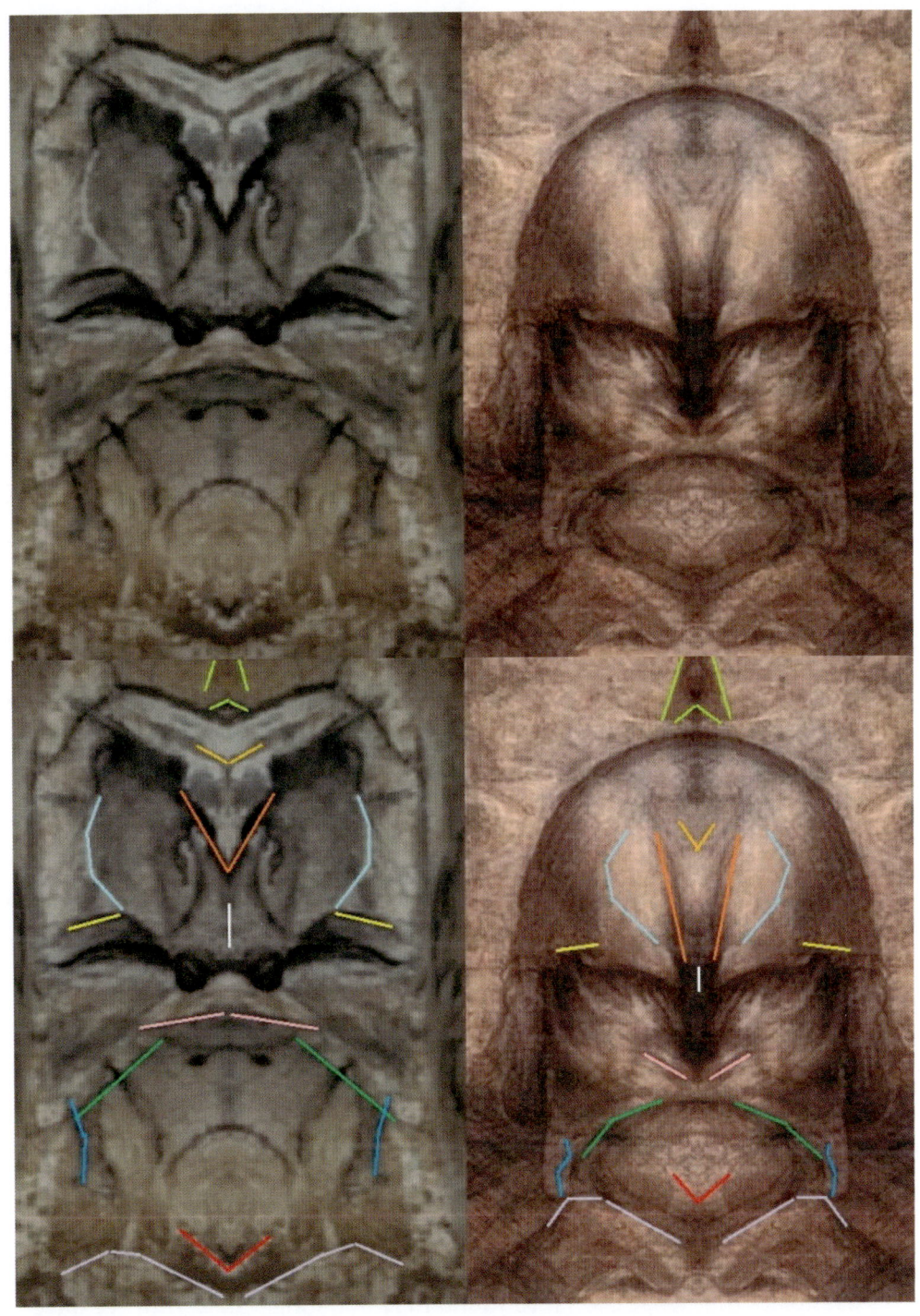

The general 'attitude of the two is striking and upon closer inspection there are at least twelve items with which to be able to compare.

Firstly, both of them are mirror images, created on the direct vertical. This means that no other manner of manipulation is required, ie, rotation or stretching or trying to make things fit in order to get a result.

But one is 30,000 years old, or so, and the other created quite recently in respect. So what made Leonardo create such an image? Did he really find almost the same type of art in another cave?

If there is such a cave that just happens to contain a copy of the Chauvet art, has Leonardo given us the clues to find it?

Some believe this cave was in the mountains just North of his home town, whilst others think it may be much closer to his home.

Some of his works contain various rock formations. Are these pointers?

"In Leonardo's earliest paintings we see the remarkable attention given to the small landscapes of the background, with lakes and water, swathed in a misty light. In the larger of the Annunciation paintings is a town on the edge of a lake. Although distant, the mountains can be seen to be scored by vertical strata. This characteristic can be observed in other paintings by Leonardo, and closely resembles the mountains around Lago di Garda and Lago d'Iseo in Northern Italy. It is a particular feature of both the paintings of The Virgin of the Rocks, which also include caverns of fractured, tumbled, and water-eroded limestone"

http://en.wikipedia.org/wiki/Science_and_inventions_of_Leonardo_da_Vinci

There is now a mission to find out. Preperations are being made to go and see if this cave can be found and what may be inside it.

Will the art lead to the caves entrance? Could it be a wild goose chase? Could we stumble upon another cave that is void of anything? There is also the possibility that what Leonardo found may no0 longer exist, but we have to try.

We have to find out.

There must be a reason as to why these two faces above are so very similar. I find it hard how this could be by chance. There is, of course, that possibility but I would not even be able to work out the odds of this happening.

Just as a point to note, in certain courts of law, a fingerprint found at a crime scene, for example, and being used for comparison, must have at least 12 matching points in order to reach a verdict. I wonder how the scientific community would fare against such measurement of these two images if this were a legal matter.

Chapter 6 Deeper into Egypt

There are other items in the paintings that caught my eye. Some took a bit of research to work out exactly what it was I was looking at, then there was the odd item that just seemed so out of place that it could not possibly be what I thought it was, yet there it is, in the painting. Nobody has touched this place in over 20,000 years since it was sealed, so just how did these people have knowledge of such things?

Perhaps we have been so blind to how the ancient cultures passed their knowledge on that we now fail to believe that what we see could be what it is. We have rough ideas and have attributed dates to such things as pottery and wine making, but occasionally, there is a spanner thrown into the works that upsets everything we thought we knew.

Let's begin with Egyptian wine making, well maybe not so much the making of wine, but more along the lines of the pottery to hold the wine or other items.

"The first evidence of wine brewing appeared on the stoppers of wine jars from the Predynastic and Thinite periods". (approx. 3,000BC)

Stoppers of wine jars! Very interesting!

According to what we know, pottery is prehistoric (before written records, basically) some of the earliest known pottery vessels date back to 20,000 BP and were discovered in Xianrendong cave in Jiangxi, China. Then there is a Venus figurine, a statuette of a nude female figure dated to 29,000–25,000 BCE (Gravettian industry). Apparently, "The early inhabitants of Europe developed pottery at about the same time as in the Near East, circa 5500–4500 BCE."

So what exactly could be in the cave paintings that relates to any of this? Here we see some ancient Egyptian wine jars;

Rather nice considering their age and obviously required some skill in order to produce items with this sort of quality. But these have a slight difference from what we see in the painting. Firstly, the necks are a bit shorter and there are no 'stoppers' to seal the jars. But we wouldn't expect to find stoppers as they may have rotted away many years ago.

What is in the painting is so very similar that it might even be possible that the artist has attempted to hide the image by smudging one edge so that it is not immediately obvious, which seems to be a recurring theme in the cave, painting things but not exactly as they are in order to throw off the scent.

The artist has given shading to the neck of the jar and has also run their finger/brush across the main body of the jar in order to give it the rounded shape we see in the photo of the Egyptian jars above. The red line is the outline of the stopper. You can see on the right side of the painted jar how extra white paint has been added to the edge in order to break the image up. The use of clever distractions like this are really acts of genius considering the message these people were trying to say.

There is one other possible item this could be. It could be a battery. There is the idea that the ancient Egyptians had some form of electric lighting, and it may be that containers of this type held acids that produced current when combined with certain metals. The complete set-up is known as The Dendera Light bulb

"Beneath the Temple of Hathor at Dendera there are inscriptions depicting a bulb-like object which some have suggested is reminiscent of a "Crookes tube" (an early light bulb). Inside the "bulbs" a snake forms a wavy line from a lotus flower (the socket of the bulb). A "wire" leads to a small box on which the air god is kneeling. Beside the bulb stands a two-armed djed pillar, which is connected to the snake, and a baboon bearing two knives. In "The Eyes of the Sphinx", Erich Von Däniken suggested that the snake represented the filament, the djed pillar was an insulator, and the tube was in fact an ancient electric light bulb. The baboon was apparently a warning that the device could be dangerous if not used correctly".

We see these jars in the picture below, although these are a modern day replica, it does not take too far of a stretch of the imagination to see how they could have been applied. There is one other object that was discovered that may also be a 'linking clue'. It is known as the Baghdad Battery.

1. Priest
2. ionized fumes
3. electric discharge (snake)
4. Lamp socket (Lotos)
5. Cable (Lotos stem)
6. Air god
7. Isolator (Djed-Pillar)
8. Light bringer Thot with knifes
9. Symbol for "current"
10. Inverse polarity (Haarpolarität +)
11. Energy storage (electrostatic Generator?)

Was this form of lighting actually in use in the cave when the paintings were applied? There is evidence of fires and charcoal left in the cave, but exactly how much? It seems incredible that the paintings were done completely by the light of little oil lamps and wood fires. How much soot is on the ceiling of the cave? Could this help to answer this question? The paintings must have taken a good period of time to complete and may have been near impossible to do with flickering flames. We must also consider how the artists moved around the cave walls in order to find the angles they were looking for in order to paint these pictures. There are several images that need to be aligned in order to see the whole image, or the hidden message.

The art was not painted, it was planned.

On another section of wall, near a single rhino that appears to be stood on a terrain with low hills painted in the background, there is a rather faint image of what looks like a man holding a pot that is about half the size of the jars. It also appears that the man is lifting the pot off of a bigger item, a table or something, yet it looks like a solid block rather than having legs. The man and 'pot' are a bit hard to see possibly due to the lighting or camera angle or the image has faded somehow. It may have been etched into the cave wall and the image we see is the actual surface rather than paint. Only a more focussed view during a return to the cave can answer this and many other questions.

The man is on the left and the rounded vase is just above centre whilst the V shaped 'table' is taking up the centre right area of the image.

The deeper we look at the paintings and at the ancient Egyptians we start to see more similarities to connect the two together.

In the Lascaux cave paintings we see many animals of various types spread along the walls or painted over each other at different angles and at varying degrees of visibility.

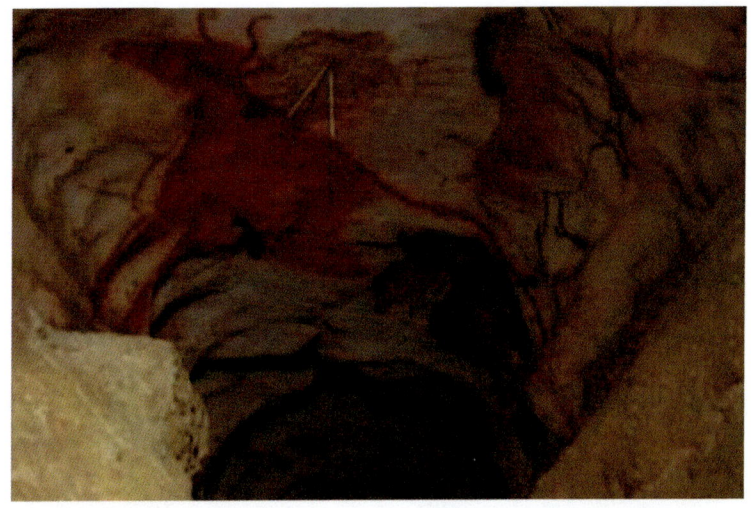

This second image of the cows was cleverly edited for the documentary "Lascaux, the prehistory of art" and you can see how the images are placed almost randomly on top of each other with no real intent in mind. It's as though they had the idea for staggering the cattle, but just did not have the full concept as to why it was done.

At Chauvet, some of the animals are repeated, or staggered, on top of each other. It's been suggested that this is to show movement. In some places this is the case but in other pictures it is to represent numbers, like a herd.

The rhino's painted along with the 'explosion' is a prime example.

We can clearly see multiple horns and bodies of the same animal. So how does this connect us to the Egyptians? They used the exact same manner of expressing multiples as we see in the cave;

It does make you wonder how a 'mid-era' set of cave paintings did not use the same staggering technique, when a much later culture arrives to use a much earlier method. How did the earlier method get carried through almost 20,000 years or more, yet bypass the 10,000 years that separated Chauvet from the Egyptians?

If the Chauvet paintings were a secret knowledge known only to the high ranking or 'elders' then why is it that such a simple thing as staggering images in that way was also passed down the line? A tiny detail, yet it connects in a way that no other seems to do.

The next item found in the paintings leads us not just to the Egyptians, but to various other cultures around the world and is a common theme. It has been presented in various forms, either as a picture or written about in texts. [The tree of life](#) has connections to many things including religion and science along with mythology and philosophy for example. "It alludes to the interconnection of all life on our planet and serves as a metaphor for common descent in the evolutionary sense.

Take note of this evolutionary theme as we will be touching on this a bit later with a couple of other images.

The 'tree of life' in the painting is at an angle on the nose of a black cow or bull (this bull may actually be hiding a further image to be shown later) which is on one of the other wall panels. It is on the panel with the four horses. The bull's horns form the actual tree itself whilst being surrounded by an archway, which is typical for this image. We see it here in the left side of this picture whilst we can see what appear to be mountains painted in the background. Perhaps they are landmarks or pointers to something else as they do not immediately give off any further 'clues'.

One of the horns branches out and adds further to the impression of a real tree. Don't you just love the way they have hidden everything? There is even shading on the inside of the arch as though to suggest this may lead somewhere. The horn with the branches seems to grow from the inside to the outside, whilst the horn in front appears to grow into the archway. The front horn also looks as though it has a root system, as you would expect to see on any tree, where it has bedded itself into the ground.

This is a tree of life from Sumer;

And here is an Aztec and Egyptian;

Looking back at the cave 'tree' we see it is sat on a blackened base. This base is carried on to the right of the picture but is stepped across a natural rock line. You can clearly see how the two levels do not match.

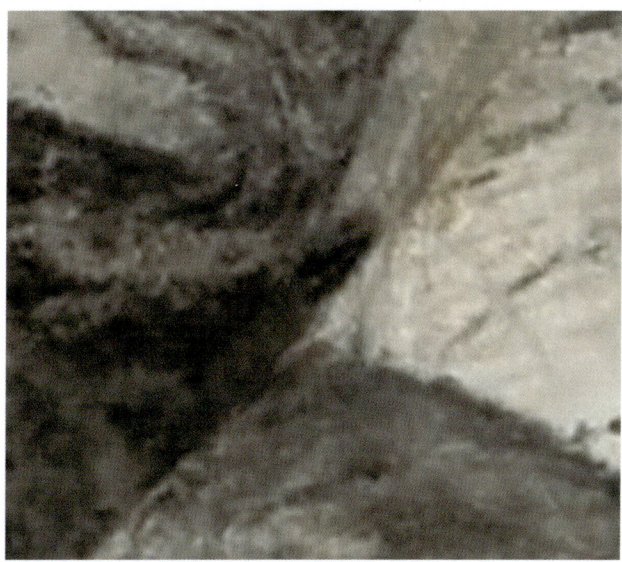

This is due to the unique way the artists were painting. They knew exactly what they were doing and had it all carefully planned out. From one angle, and distance, the complete picture looks just like they intended, a bull with horns. But at another angle you get to see something else;

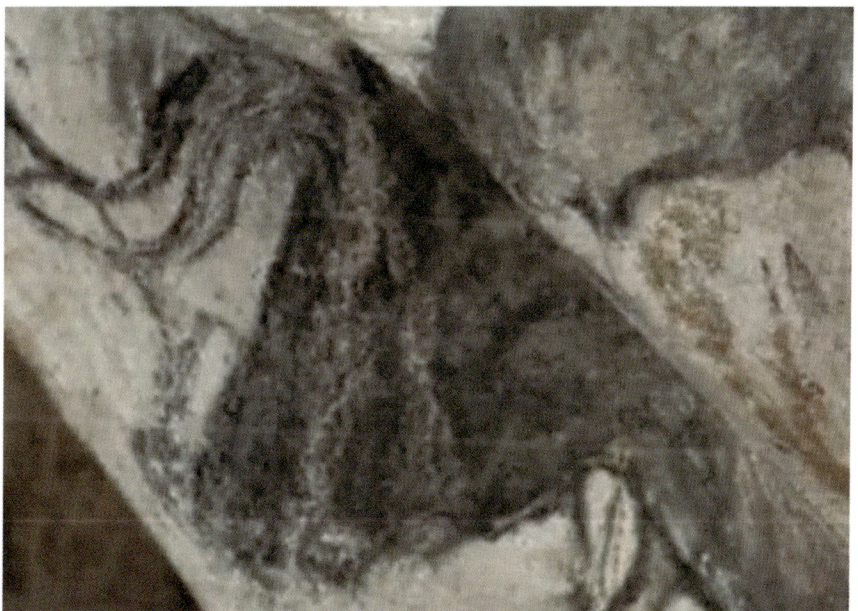

A black Pyramid!

The 'tree of life' archway is sat right on this Pyramid. Is there not a two inch hole in the side of a Pyramid that is said to be aimed at the stars and that it allows the soul to travel back and forth? Are the archway and Pyramid in the cave trying to tell us something? Was it a plan for a future development or had this one particular Pyramid already been built? Maybe it is associated with another Pyramid somewhere and not necessarily any of the ones at or around Giza.

Makes you wonder!

We know that the some surfaces of the cave were prepared before painting. This involved the scraping away of an area in order to reveal the much whiter rock underneath. This is apparent when you view from a distance and some edges are rather straight and well defined. There is one section that has been cleared to almost be square.

In this small box, some of the original surface has been left behind. As I mentioned before, this is one of the techniques used to build up parts of other images. This one, though, appears to be more of a set of hieroglyphs rather than anything else. I am in no way an expert on such things so this could be just what I think I'm seeing until it is proven to be otherwise. The point being that it is what I have observed and am including it here in order for it to be recorded and noted.

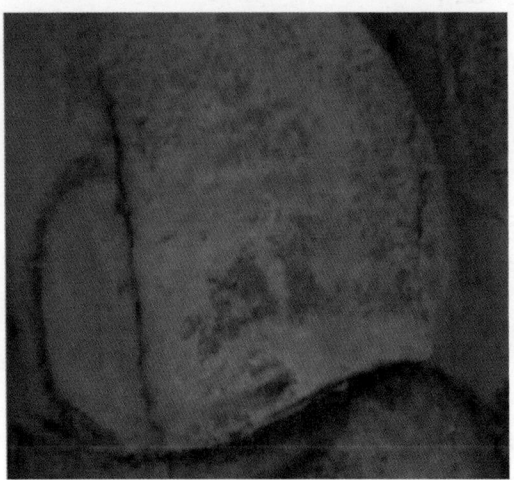

The 'square' is a bit rough, but it is possible to see that there might be some attempt to create something here. It looks like three glyphs, the lowest one being a 'question mark' shape, above that a line and above that an oval shape.

Here is a close up section of the markings;

Perhaps this set of hieroglyph meanings is the wrong set, or had advanced in a way that the above becomes unreadable, but you can see how the image made me think;

```
A 𓃀 or —    H 𓎡 or 🗆   O 𓅱    V 𓃛
B 𓃭         I 𓇌        P 🗆    W 𓅱
C 𓂝 or 𓏏   J 𓂝        Q 𓂧    X 𓂝 𓏏
D 𓂧         K 𓂝        R 𓂝    Y 𓏭 or \\
```

Update Edit

Ancient North African Rivers

New evidence of rivers in North Africa previously known by the Chauvet cave artists.

As you may already know from my book or previous posts, there is a panel of art in the Chauvet cave that I believe represents North Africa. I have also mentioned before as to how clever the art is and how it overlaps itself and each part has multiple meanings. This map is no exception. It has several layers built into it and appears to show knowledge of the area at different periods of time.

With a report published on the 11th September, this begins to reveal the 'map' theory in greater detail and brings about further discoveries that must be more than simple coincidence. There are far too many of these coincidences going on in this incredible piece of work.

The new report come from the PLOS journal, PLOS ONE and asks "Were Rivers Flowing across the Sahara During the Last Interglacial?"

I have to say yes due to what I have known for the last 8 months or so.

What have I found that backs up this research? I'm not going to go into a long winded write up, I'm going to get right into it..

In these two images, we see the rivers as predicted by the research, next to it is a portion of the cave art that represents the same area (and which I also believe represents the Nile delta too) We are looking at the three main arteries of river in both pictures. There is one detail in particular that strongly suggests that what we are seeing is in fact true. Take a look at the middle river in the cave art, follow it down until the end where you can see it splits off into two small lines. The middle river from the research project also does this. They both end in the same way, by branching off in the same directions.

If we take a look at the far left river in the art, we can see how it 'feathers' out at the bottom which ties in with the way the research river has lots of smaller river and streams coming off the end of it and a sourced by the mountain range. If we look up this same left river to near the 'elbow' we can see that just to the left of that are two Y shaped lines that are also part of the river system as we see in the research map.

Going over to the river on the far right, we see how it forms into a long narrow V shape before becoming a trailing line. The long V shape is comparable to the vast network of smaller rivers and streams that make up this section on the research map. These examples can only mean two things.

1. The research about the ancient rivers is correct.

2. The idea that this bit of art in the cave is a map is correct.

The two confirm each other. 30,000 years apart, but they're still correct. There is something else about this cave map that I will touch on afterwards.

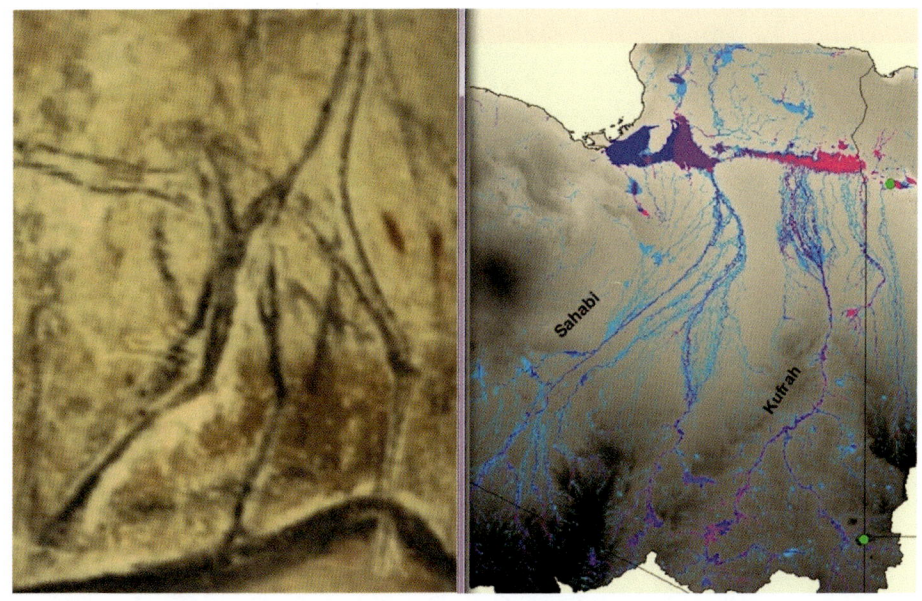

    In these next image we can see the scale of both maps and how very similar a lot of the other rivers are to each other, although there does seem to be a few from the cave art that are not appearing on the research map. There is another one that is rather faintly drawn but that line does match up with the river over on the far left which runs down almost over the entirity of that side. On the cave art we see two strongly drawn lines that also branch out rather slightly on their ends suggestive of smaller rivers and streams connecting to them.

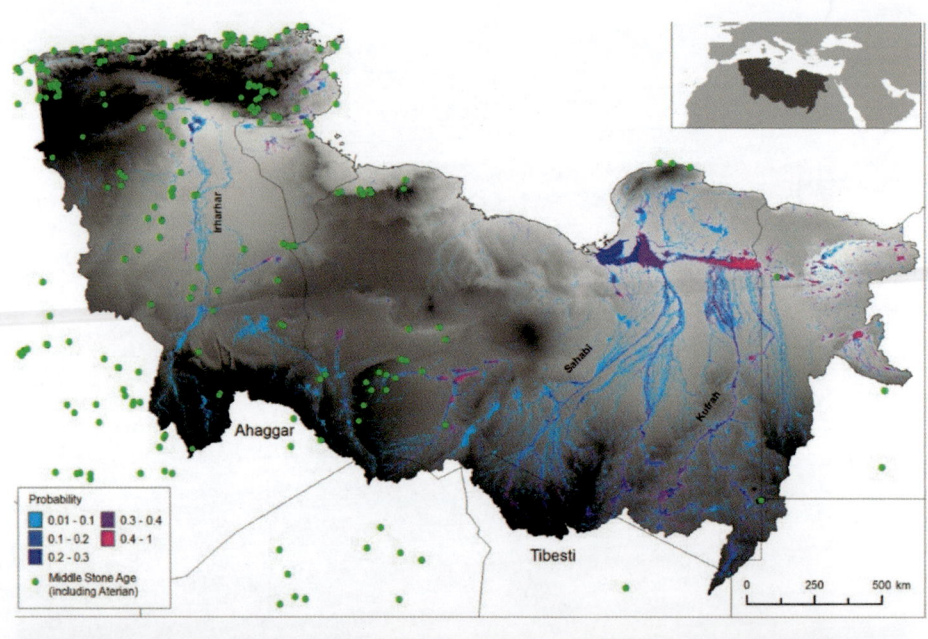

And here are the three circles found in the rough location of where the cave art represents them. Take note of their alignment in comparison to those on the art.

It was brought to my attention that these markings are on 19.5 degrees. Credit for this goes to Barry Flanagan. You can all check to see just how close to the exact 19.5 degrees the central point of these three circles are or you can check this image below. The fdark lines I have drawn may not be as exact as they could be, but the actual marker point of the 19.5 degrees does appear to be pretty special due to the location and connection to the cave art and other things.

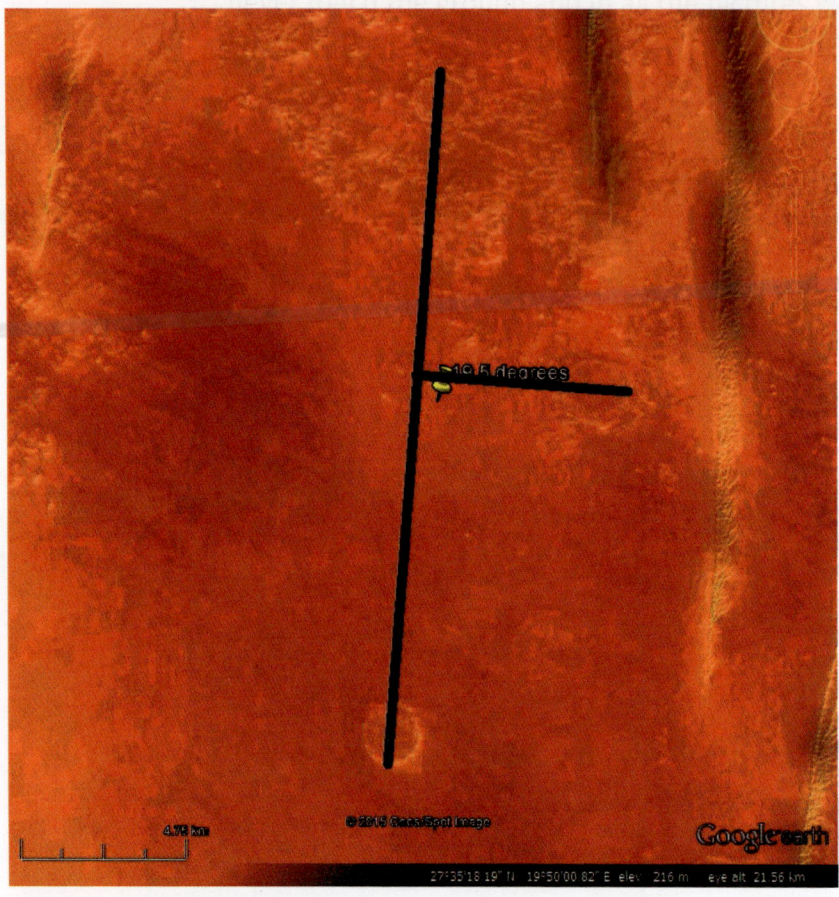

For those who have no idea as to the relevance of this positioning, Then please take a moment to read this..

"It has been found to be associated with various ancient structures here on earth – Giza pyramids, Avebury (the largest stone circle in the world, near Stonehenge), Pyramids of the Sun and Moon at Teotihuacan, etc. It is also worth noting that the Egyptian hieroglyph for Sirius, the brightest star in the sky which was extremely important to ancient Egyptians, is an equilateral triangle which can be viewed as a 2-dimensional representation of a tetrahedron; and in the Egyptian translation, it means a doorway... a sort of 'stargate'. Curiously, it has also been observed that 19.5 degrees is closely linked, for some reason, with the NASA space missions (for example, Mars Pathfinder landed at 19.5

degrees lat. of Mars on July 4, '97). In fact, not only did Pathfinder landed at 19.5 N, the longitude of the landing site was approximately 33 W – which is the very number of the longitude of the apex of the Great Bend of the Nile (33 E)! Now, this strongly insists on the relevance of the Nile numbers"

http://www.vortexmaps.com/planets.php

And I'm sure you will also be able to find loads more info on the 19.5 degrees elsewhere on the net should you so wish to learn more. A search for Richard Hoagland will help you on that journey.

Chapter 7 Ra, the creative power!

The meaning behind the name Ra is uncertain yet it has managed to have a form of connection to 'creator' or 'creative power'.

Perhaps there is more to this than we think. Could it be that Ra was so knowledgeable in the matters of life, death and how planets and creatures evolve, that he became connected to this through his ability to demonstrate such matters? Was the ancient Egyptian art of mummification a slightly twisted attempt at recreating some of Ra's skills? Could it be that the message became confused over 30,000 years.

The boats that Ra used to take his journey through the sky and the duat, the underworld, were known as the Mandjet (the boat of millions of years or morning boat) and Mesektet (evening boat). So what is the Mandjet all about? Where did the idea of millions of years come from? A measure of knowledge about life, the stars and everything must have influenced this idea. Knowing that things had been, and would be, going on for millions, if not billions, of years would have made quite an impression on such an early culture. Today, it's the sort of thing we learn in school, along with computers and various other levels of science and study them side by side with dinosaur fossils. With Ra's advanced knowledge he could explain the workings of the solar system and how the Earth rotates and moves around the Sun, hence becoming a master or controller of them by a group of people with limited understanding.

There was a belief that Ra wept and from the tears man was created. To us today, that sounds very much like the extraction of DNA from a donated liquid and using the DNA to build a species (have you seen the film Prometheus? – similar type of principle in a way)

In the book of the dead, Ra cuts himself and his blood transforms into two personifications. One was authority, the other was mind. Maybe the lesson here is to keep control of your mind as it is powerful and can be used for the wrong thing (corruption, wanting to be the boss of all, war, greed etc.). The blood could be symbolic that we're all human and we must share this planet together and learn to become that which we have always aimed to be, better than we currently are!

In the film [Stargate](), we see a 'Ra' that has enslaved the citizens of a planet. Ra is some alien creature that took on human form. This version though seems to be a bit too far away from the Ra we may be seeing here, yet the Stargate Ra is extremely powerful and has knowledge beyond the level of those he has enslaved. When we see a representation like that, it is easy to see how such a person could become connected to almost everything you'd ever known.

I often wonder how we would be perceived by people if we were to travel back several thousand years. Would we be seen as some form of magician or a God? Trying to explain ourselves and our 'abilities' would be difficult as we may not be understood and our words would get twisted.

There are two images in the cave that made me think along the lines of evolution, or at least, the knowledge of evolution. Firstly, there is the image of the bird-man. He is not alone. There are a few other images blended in with him that, to me, look very similar to something that we use in order to represent the evolutionary ladder.

At first, the image does not look like much apart from what I've already shown, but look again and you'll notice that there are two outlines of similarly shaped creatures that appear to be moving along in a similar fashion, but there is a hint of difference to them. Don't forget the artists 'stagger' their images of animals, but the staggered creatures here are not the same. The last outline has raised its head (near top-left of picture). Then, the one between that and the bird-man does not appear to have a long nose but its leg is decidedly different (below bird-man's stomach).

Next we come to the one image that is not of any of these three creatures. There is a human arm with a hand that is reaching out as if to grab something. It reaches out from under the bird-man's chin (as if from behind) and crosses over the bird-man's nose. The arm and hand are also painted in a much brighter colour than anything around it, drawing attention to it.

So what do we know that could be anywhere near similar to what we see above? Maybe something like this;

What else is in the cave that could possibly back this up and give it any chance of being considered?

On the panel where the four horses are, there are two rhino fighting, but the photo also contains a tiny portion of another panel and it is in this little piece that I saw something that, again, left me rather shocked.

Here is the panel in question. It is in the top right corner that is of interest to us. From here it does not look much, but cropped and zoomed it is rather different. I would love to get up close to this bit of work.

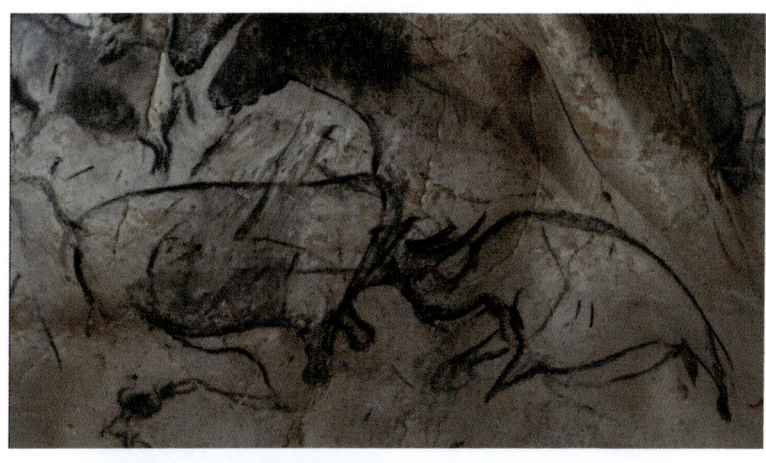

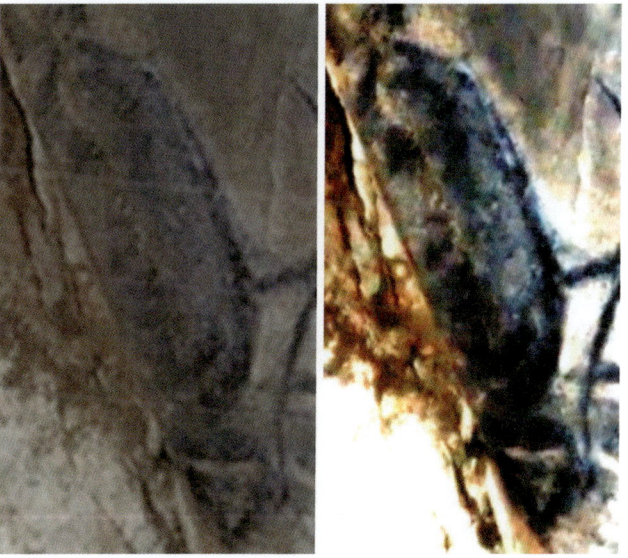

Two versions of the same thing but one has been brightened to try to bring out a bit more detail. Really needs a proper photograph of it though.

What we may be looking at is a half fish-half man creature. The fishes head takes up most of the image, but there is a left leg, bent at the knee, and a left arm, both in a position as if to suggest climbing or crawling. If you look closely at what would be the posterior, there is a tail curling around the body.

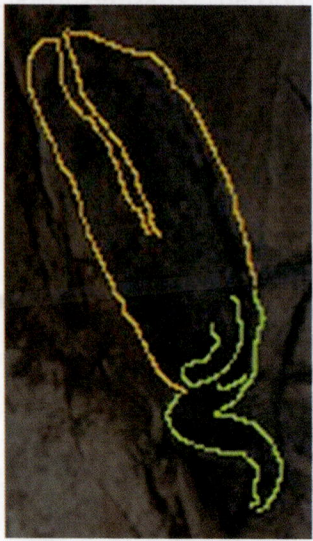

Can we be certain that the cave artists were so simple that all they could draw were horses, lions and rhino? Are we so sure of ourselves that there was not some very advanced knowledge being shared way back into our past? Did they learn about evolution and many other things, yet it was forgotten or changed and twisted by the warped minds of those who wanted to keep this knowledge secret in order to control the rest of a population?

Perhaps the answer is in the caves, or another one, as there are some things in the cave I just have not been able to work out yet.

Maybe there is more in the art that we have not really touched upon properly or are not looking at correctly. Earlier, I used a mirroring method to present an entire face. I thought this might be worth trying on other portions of the art work and one image I found is rather interesting.

In keeping with the theme of some creational force and legends of devices used to hold or contain certain items of power, we see here, in this mirrored image, a set of lions looking at, from several angles, a chalice or grail, a cup of some description.

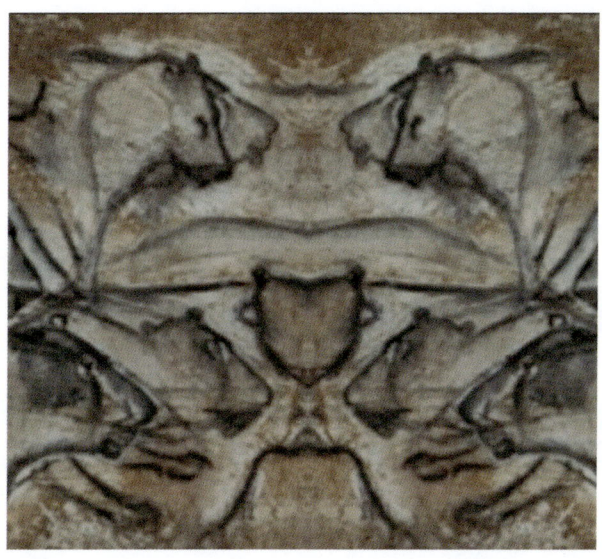

Then, just when you think you've seen it all with regards to some form of ancient connection or 'word of mouth' secret that gets passed along the line by one elder to the next via secret handshakes and nods of the head we find yet another obvious link to the cave art. On the church of Maria Saal, Carinthia, Austria, there is a Roman relief of two 'lions rampant', guarding a chalice or vase or grail whilst the tree of life grows from it.

Could the legend of the Holy Grail go further back in time than our current history have us believe? Has the hunt for the grail gone on just as long?

Update edit

The REAL da Vinci code

The Annunciation by Leonardo da Vinci holds a secret.

It holds an image of the Holy Grail and shows two trees growing out of the cup.

There are a few important points to be aware of here, firstly take note that the angel has one hand lowered and one raised. The stem of the bookstand on the pedestal is not centralised, it is slightly over to the left side of the pedestal. This painting is yet another connection to an ancient past where da Vinci appears to be showing his knowledge of.

As I have shown before, the Chauvet cave art contains certain sections where, if mirrored on the direct vertical, a secondary image can be found (it's a bit more detailed than that). Here we find this method used in da Vinci's work yet again

Leonardo painted the book stand off-centre so that it could be met in the middle like this. Please notice that in the original, the pedestal has two flowers on the lower section. Once mirrored, these two flowers become one flower below the bookstand. This is a key to this mirror method. It's like a marker or guiding point, deliberate intent. We now see a winged person with one hand lowered, one hand raised on either side of a grail form. We can also see two trees growing from the grail. On either side of the trees are two mounds. These are also a connecting 'link'.

We can now see a Roman relief from Austria. We see two lions guarding a chalice which has two trees twisting around each other and growing from the cup. Both lions have one paw on the floor and one paw raised.

Next, St. Marks, Venice. Winged horses, one hoof raised, two trees entwined growing from a cup.

Syrian goblet. Winged humanoids, one hand lowered, one raised

Aztec and Egyptian

And Chauvet, lions guarding the grail, one paw lowered, one raised.. notice the two mounds directly above the grail form. This image also depicts birth of first Egyptian god, Ra.

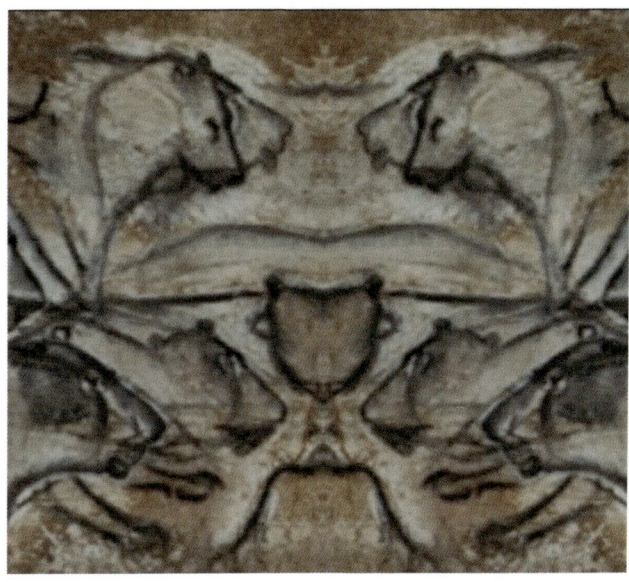

The Holy Grail was never a physical "cup", it is the DNA, the bloodline, the family tree of a distant relative from over 35,000 years ago!

Finally, modern heraldry... depicting a family tree with lion and winged dragon 'rampant' (one leg low, other up high), mouths open and tongue sticking out (as we see in the hippo from earlier).

So, as I've said before with the humanoid face found in the cave art and Leonardo's art, just what did he know? Where did he get this information from? did he discover a copy of the Chauvet art in another cave and why was he compelled to hide all of this in his work?

You would have thought that something like the Holy Grail would have been an important topic to paint, but it would appear that it is one of those types of secrets that has had its story twisted over time. What was secret became a talked about topic and then was finally used in the Biblical version of the Grail story when, in fact, it relates to something that is over 35,000 years old..

Chapter 8 The Unknown

For someone who lived 1,000 years ago, these cave paintings may not have seemed like much else but animals. Even 500 years ago it might have been a struggle to get past a vast majority of the images. 100 years ago you may have been laughed at, but even now there may be images in the paintings that are not fully understood by our minds as we just do not yet have the knowledge to fully understand what we are seeing.

If it was not for satellite imaging of the Earth, we may never have seen the 'eye of Ra' which is the crater near Tehran, nor the lioness north-East of it. Yes, we might have been able to work out the map of Africa and the Mediterranean due to our ability to sail the seas and create maps, but that might have been as far as we had gotten.

We have been extremely lucky in finding the caves. Being able to sit and examine them on a computer screen from our armchair is a miracle in itself. The images have been painted with incredible skill and technique. They talk to us in a way that only our level of knowledge and understanding can recognise. We need to look at them in the right light, at the correct angle and with an open mind in order to see what is there.

A few things are puzzling me though. One panel seems to be painted solely for a particular angle of view. It looks like it has a background of block work. There are lines that look staggered as if you were seeing a brick or stone wall. In front of this are a few animals, but there is also the impression of flames. One set of flames are drawn as you would draw the flame of a candle. The other set is either natural colouring of the rock, in this case orange, or it was painted on. Either way, it looks like a flaming wall of rock. Could it be that this is telling us about some form of destruction by fire? It's hard to say as I have not been able to see this picture in its proper alignment.

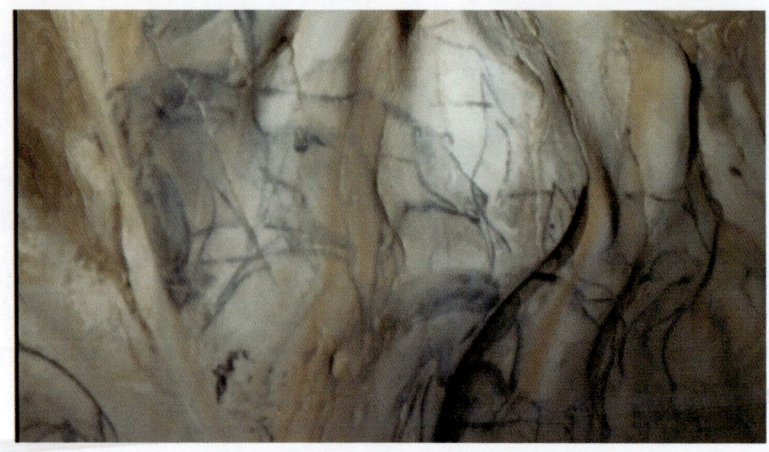

Another item reminds me of a Knights helmet, but it just does not yet make any sense to me as to what it is or what it could represent. It is found on a panel with a horse, deer and antelope. I think you can see how it reminds me of a 'Knights' helmet. The bottom curve is where it would sit on your shoulders, sloping upwards into the neck piece and finally filling out into the face plate and helm section. Either way, I don't get this one… yet!

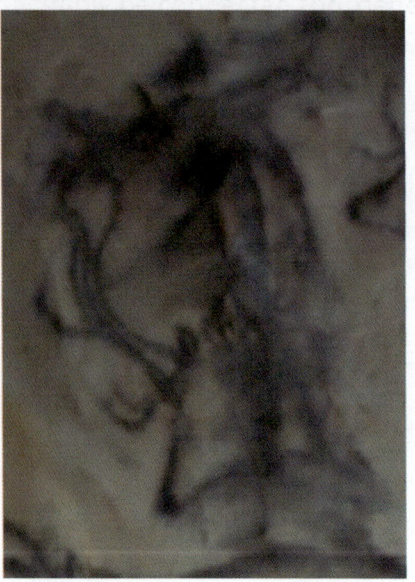

This next side-by-side image has made me wonder if there is a place somewhere near Baghdad that has not yet been discovered. The rhino image from the cave (on the right) is so similar to an aerial view of the Baghdad region that you can even see the location of a rvier in both images. The ears of the rhino are part of the terrain as well as the horn. Like before, it was the red spots that led me to find this comparison on earth. It's rather stunning how the river seems to have hardly changed direction in all that time if this is what I think it is trying to show.

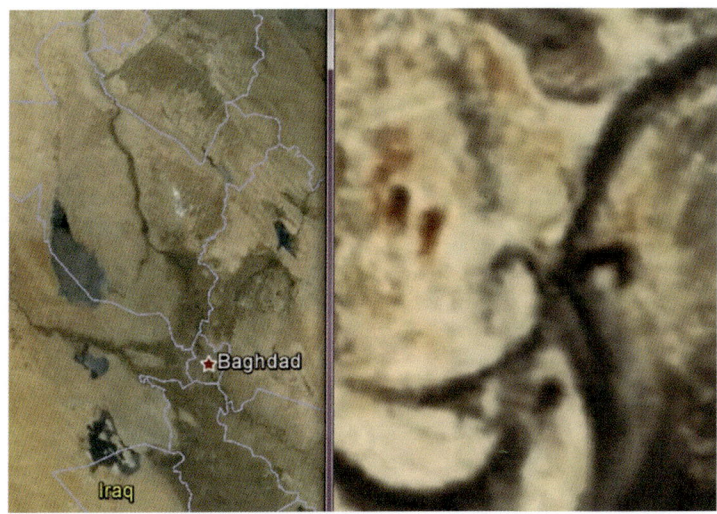

And finally, we come to a piece that was in the start of the documentary, a piece that was set up on a wall, all on its own. It is described as being some kind of insect but it may be something else. It's the oddest looking insect I've ever seen and it has a brother.

But the brother is approximately 10,000 years younger!

Here is the 'insect' from Chauvet;

And now you'll see another painting of this 'insect', but please realise that part of the cave ceiling that it was painted on has come away over time and only about 3/4s of the image is left, but you can still say the two are almost identical in design. To explain the suggested 10,000 year gap, this 'insect' is in the Lascaux cave;

From what I can see, there appears to be only one of these in each cave.

We have a connection here, a connection that spans 30,000 years, visits several different caves, touches lands that span the globe and leads us through the lives of many cultures, taking us all the way to the very tip of one of the most amazing civilisations we've ever known, the ancient Egyptians.

I would love to see a return visit to the Chauvet cave to get as many pictures as possible. I am interested in the use of a 'full-spectrum' video camera with IR and UV lighting just in case there is something mixed in with the paint that may reveal more. If they were so clever to hide all this, I can only imagine what else they may have hidden. To say these people were primitive is an insult to them, they have proven that they were far and beyond anything we previously believed. They, or someone, were obviously highly intelligent and highly skilled.

Some of the mirror images I've been looking at reveal some very interesting results, but they are not definitive and I am yet to discover anything that I can relate them to or confirm them with, so they are safely locked away until a time where they make sense or have something credible for me to match them to and bring them out into the open. For example, there is this 'Jackal' but it is not as fine as we see in anything Egyptian. This could be due to the artist's technique and skill when they created the image, yet we can see how it could possibly be a version of this type of animal.

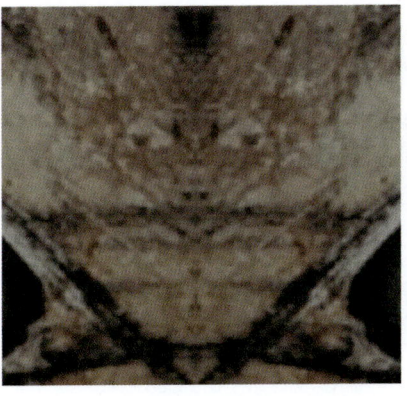 

On the surface of Mars lies a mound of, well, Mars! Can't quite say a mound of earth! But this is no ordinary mound of Mars. This mound has a design to it. It is a design that can only be compared to one earthly image, the eye of Horus. Or the eye of Ra as some prefer, but they are almost the same thing as they represent two forms of the same deity.

Horus is one of the oldest and most significant deities in ancient Egyptian religion and the symbol that most relates to him is known around the world. He is either seen as the eye we know or as a bird of prey, there is doubt over exactly which one, it's either a falcon or a hawk or he is seen as a bird headed man. He is also associated with Mars!

Now there's a surprise!

"…the Egyptian God HORUS is identical with planet MARS. And that means that all the Gods inside of the myth are celestial bodies, in the same way as in the Epic of Creation. So this myth describes a very special cosmic event."

http://www.bibliotecapleyades.net/marte/esp_marte_18.htm

"The sky god Horus protecting the red (?) disk of Mars (NOT THE SUN!) which at this particular time was named Ramesses ('Fashioned by Re'), personified here as the young king. Photo credit: Jon Bosworth"

http://www.gks.uk.com/Horus-falcon-god/

So what has this all got to do with the face on Mars and the potential of it being a real representation of what everyone thinks it is, a face? How does the mirroring of it, and showing a lions face, fit into this picture as well? What else do we need to help us prove that what we see is what we have really got?

We need more things that can actually connect in such a way that there can be little room for any doubt. But even with these things, are we really happy to admit that there is a connection or is it all still so strange that we cannot yet accept it as a possible reality? These questions and many more have been flooding my head for a long time, but now, I feel more ready than ever and am discovering new connections almost on a weekly basis, as I have said before, and this week something came my way that has helped me enforce the possibilities listed above.

This picture came my way courtesy of NASA doing all the leg work and Gary Leggiere...aka...MARS REVEALER for the actual find and posting of.

This image is on the surface of Mars and it is the eye of Horus.

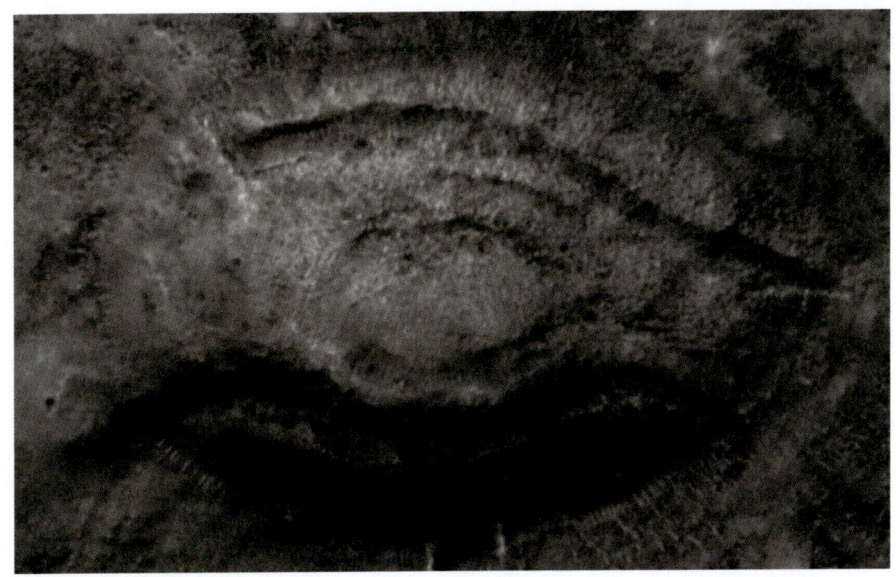

How am I so sure of that? From my findings in the Chauvet cave art, that's how. The 30,000 year old art has led me on a rather wild ride these last seven or eight months and I know it is not over yet, not by a long shot! I know there is far more to discover in the art. But what could possibly be in the art that this Martian image could relate to?

Well, obviously the eye of Horus, of course.

Now to show you the points of interest as to how these image match. There are a few pieces that give us a deeper idea as to how they 'connect'. This is more than a 'looks similar' type of match as you will see in this next set.

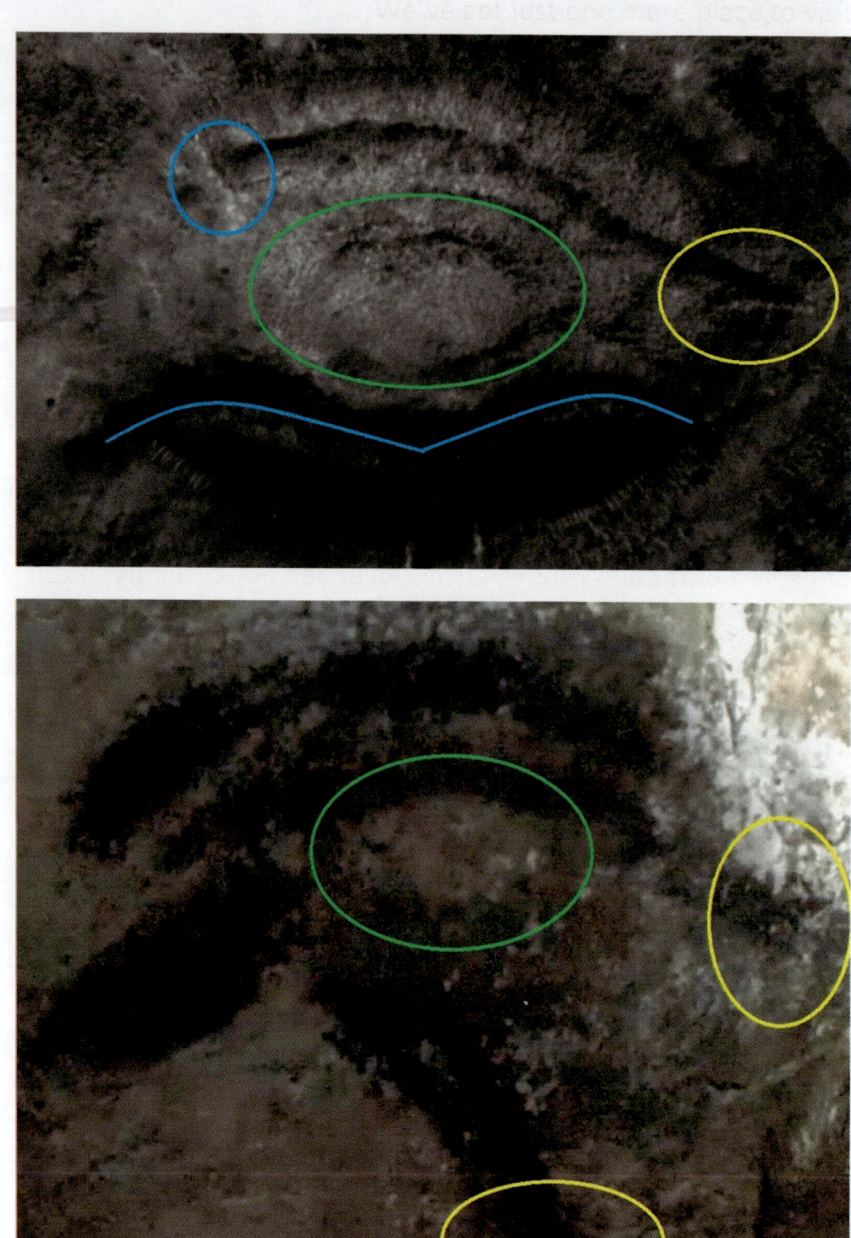

What are we exactly looking at? Firstly, the yellow circles, they are showing the 'shark tail' effect given to the art work. It is a sloping tail that ends in a point rather than the square ended version we see in the blue circle and on many other versions.

The green circle is the barely visible 'physical' eye that we see. Then, the wavy blue line is clearly seen in the last image as a matching wavy blue line. These factors placed together can only mean that the image on Mars was designed and was made to resemble something that was either from Mars or travelled to Mars via Earth or some other variation. Perhaps Earth was the final destination before departing for somewhere else and they left their mark here? The second image is 30,000 years old and can be found in the Chauvet cave art and is easily spotted.

Now we shall continue with the actual face on Mars itself and its connection to the Chauvet cave.

This face from the cave, which we saw earlier, is seen in a panel of lions and only half the face is showing, as we know.

This humanoid face is rather bizarre, yet it is there, no denying it. Why was it painted into the art? Anyway, I felt that there was something important about it being in the set of lions, and I could not work out what. Out of curiosity I turned the image upside down and found more, a lion, as you will see in this set.

Due to a lot of other things that I have found in the cave art, I realised that I may be looking at something that is not on this world. I was seeing the face on Mars. I was aware that some thought that the two mirrored halves of the Mars face created a humanoid and a lion. Well, this cave face is mirrored and has two halves, so, here in this set we see how they compare to the face on Mars. I have included one of the original versions of the face and one of the so called 'more up to date' version.

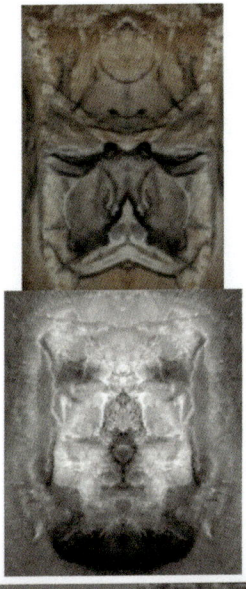
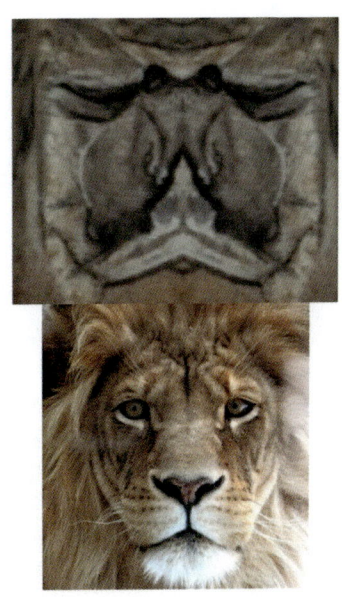
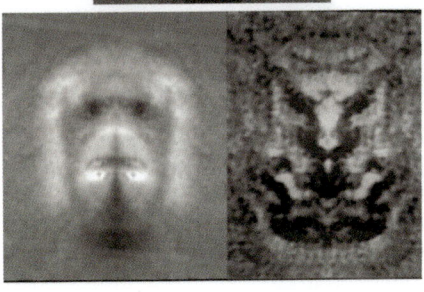

Some may think we're seeing what we want to see in land formations that have been there for millions of years, but I feel we might need to throw that idea out. If anyone was capable of travelling so far to reach two separate planets you can bet they have the skill to be able to transform terrain. As we have read earlier, this creature is actually shaped using the land itself. The point is, this can be seen from about 60km up at this scale and surely it cannot be pure luck that the hilly terrain that forms the shape is natural. Also, this creature is not alone in the area.

Can we now say that the face on Mars, and lots of other things we think we see on the surface, really are what we think we are seeing? Apart from going there, this is one of the best examples I can think of as evidence (this and the pyramids).

Update Edit

The Rampant Lion, from Chauvet to Mars...

The rampant lion appears to be a very strong, and old, image. I wont get into the where, why, when but will go directly to providing several examples that appear to all be connected in some way.

They may all be so tightly entwined with each other that we simply cannot ignore them, no matter how much their message differs. We know how stories can change over time.

So, we have this set of lions that have their front feet raised with their tails in the air. The lion rampant is still used today in modern heraldry usually guarding a shield which contains the family tree.

As you may have read, the lower right image appears to be a feline that can be seen from approximately 150kms ABOVE the Earths surface.

This is where we are now headed

Above, to Mars.

Next is an ESA Image that has had a contrast adjust and provided by Brett C. Sheppard

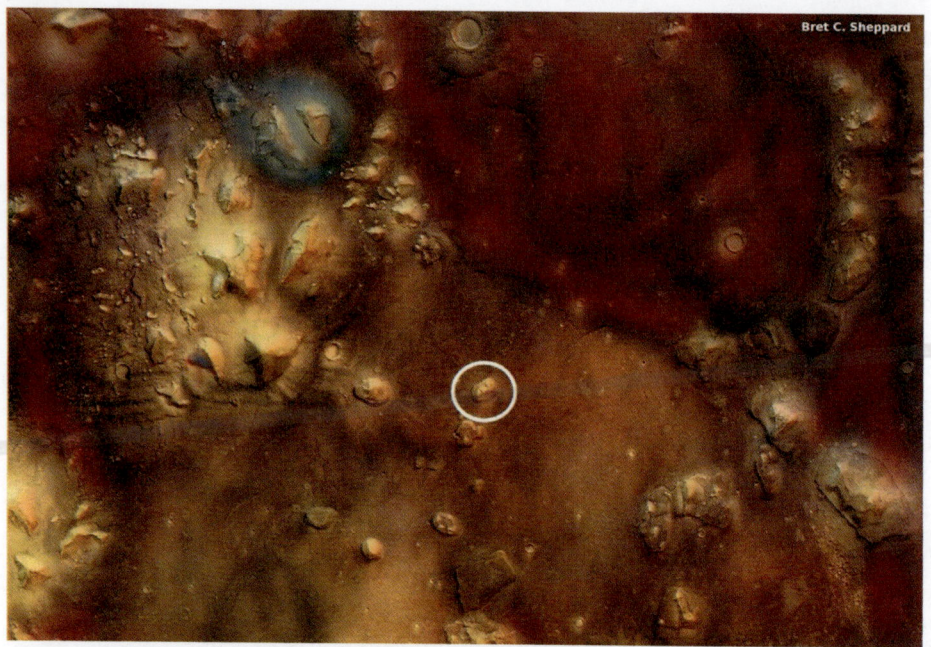

The famous face in the Cydonia region is the circled object in the centre of the image.

You would have to have your eyes closed not to notice how very much the image of a male lion stands out. I decided to highlight the outline in order to represent it better.

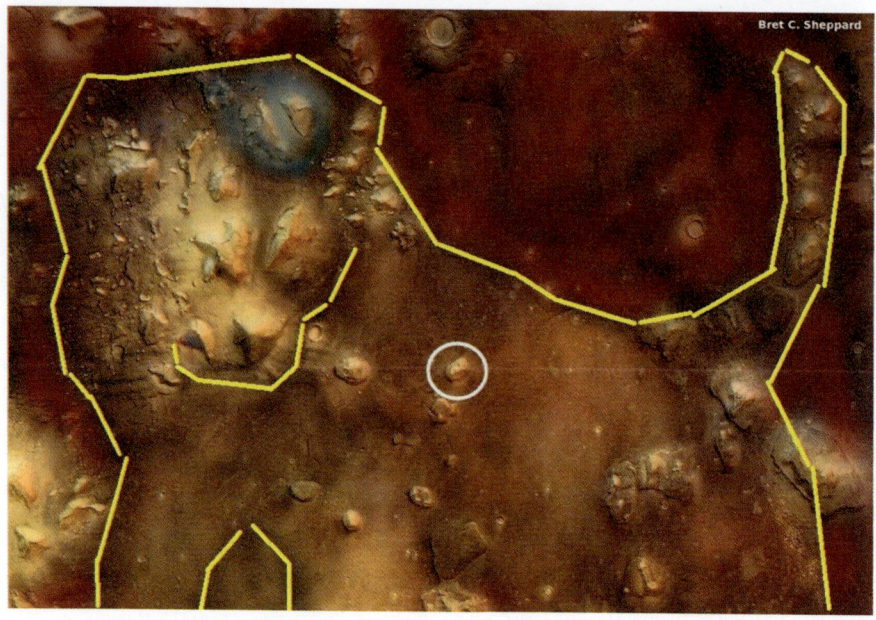

Later, I realised that there may be more to this lion and needed to have a look at a larger area so using Google Earth (Mars) I was able to pull up a wider area and I believe to have found the full lion.

And then slight adjustment of contrast and highlighted outline

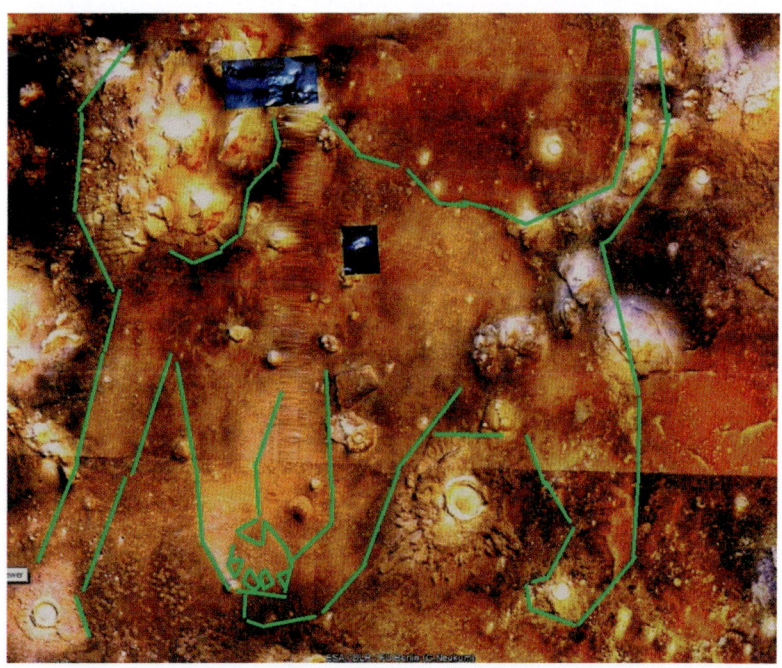

And here is the Earthly one

About the only differences between the two is that one appears to be female and is facing another direction. From theChauvet cave art, there are no lions with a mane, yet it is said that there are male lions represented in the art alongside the females. This could be an important part of the puzzle.. Why does a male lion look down from Mars to a female lion on Earth that looks the left.. the exact same direction as the lions from the Chauvet cave…

The lion on Earth looks West towards Egypt.. The lions in the cave look The same direction towards an image that appears to show a link to the ancient Egyptian culture.

What is the importance of this?

Personally, if all of the above is as multi layered with multiple meanings as the cave art of Chauvet, then it may be a while before we come up with the reasons as to why and what these images are all about.

Update Edit

Ancient Egypt's first King, the hybrid, Ra

I was discussing my book with another author and to try to encapsulate the 'message' of seperate pieces from one wall of the Chauvet cave art, I pieced together several of the images onto one to try to show the location of each individual item and its relative relation to places on Earth.

What happened next kinda knocked me off my feet a bit when I realised what this one wall may actually be saying. If it is correct, then it has effectively eluded me for a while but only because I had not read the pieces as a whole.

Here is that image. There are six sections which appear to give a message that we are all very familiar with.

Section 1;

This contains the 'map' of North Africa and the Mediterranean represented through several animals.

Section 2;

Represents the middle East and includes Baghdad, Gobekli Tepe and an area next to Namak lake, south of Tehran.

Section 3;

Is of a rather erotic image of a particular female body part/s. The left thigh can be seen as part of the art and the rock surface. The right thigh ends abruptly but they have drawn an arc across the rock to represent the form of the right thigh. I will leave the other details of this nude figure for you to work out. I don't think I need to be too specific here. This Section of the wall is the womb of the cave, the point where mother Earth is symbolised, everything that is female and life bearing.

Section 4;

Cygnus. This set represents Cygnus and Draco. For a more precise discussion on this image, which is found throughout ancient Egypt, you might like to have a read of this thread. Is this here in order to represent a particular date? Deneb is the major star of Cygnus and was once the pole star. Could that be the reason why it is here, or could there be some other meaning that relates to the stars?

Section 5;

The Chalice. This is a multi-layered image where we get to see one item with two meanings. Firstly, the 'chalice' (or grail. The Holy grail was said to contain the lifeblood of Christ) is most noticeable. The second meaning to this image represents the birth of the first Egyptian God, Ra.

Section 6;

Ra. The method of finding this image was the same for section 5 and a couple of others from the art suggesting that the method was known and deliberately inserted into the art. Here we see a humanoid figure. Could this be the face of Ra? Maybe it is something else?

So what possible message could all of this be saying?

I suggest that it is saying this…

1. 'visitors' came to Africa and settled in the Nile region.

2. Eventually they travelled Eastward and got involved in various regions whilst there.

3. A female was selected for breeding.

4. The stars pinpoint the date or location (led by Deneb) towards;

5. The birth of the first hybrid child, who;

6 Became Ra, the first King of Egypt.

Now, this is where you come in. I'm already sure we have either been visited before or were so advanced that we left this planet or a combination of the two. Now it is up to you to review the evidence and take your step forwards into what was known and what we are re-learning.

Every time I try to close this book I think of something else and how it connects to our lives and our other sections of human history, yet putting it all in here would, I feel, slowly distract from the main impact of these wonderful creations. We have had many questions asked about these paintings, now we have many more, but these same questions have also answered questions from other places in our past. The link to Seti the 1st is astonishing on its own!

An incredible cave filled with unbelievable pictures.

There is more, much more…!

Index

This list is of those that are hyperlinked in the main text. These appear in the order they are found in the main text. Most links were also used in the finding of certain images and/or information. Wikipedia has been used mainly as a guide line rather than being actual factual references. If I had used a particular scholar's research I'm sure there would have been someone who would disagree with it. My point being that should you wish to confirm anything I used from Wikipedia then please do check things out in your own studies as we know information changes all the time as people discover new things. Sometimes our history books do not get updated as fast or as frequently as we would like.

http://en.wikipedia.org/wiki/Chauvet_Cave

http://en.wikipedia.org/wiki/Cave_of_Forgotten_Dreams

http://en.wikipedia.org/wiki/Ard%C3%A8che

http://en.wikipedia.org/wiki/Aurignacian

http://en.wikipedia.org/wiki/Eye_of_Ra

http://en.wikipedia.org/wiki/Ra

http://en.wikipedia.org/wiki/All_seeing_eye

http://en.wikipedia.org/wiki/Four_Horsemen_of_the_Apocalypse

http://en.wikipedia.org/wiki/Cygnus_%28constellation%29

http://en.wikipedia.org/wiki/Marrakesh

http://en.wikipedia.org/wiki/Neolithic

http://en.wikipedia.org/wiki/Nouakchott

http://en.wikipedia.org/wiki/Richat_Structure

http://en.wikipedia.org/wiki/Tehran

http://en.wikipedia.org/wiki/Namak_Lake

http://en.wikipedia.org/wiki/Erik_von_Daniken

http://en.wikipedia.org/wiki/Chariots_of_the_Gods%3F

http://en.wikipedia.org/wiki/G%C3%B6bekli_Tepe

http://en.wikipedia.org/wiki/Southeastern_Anatolia_Region

http://en.wikipedia.org/wiki/Turkey

http://en.wikipedia.org/wiki/Michelangelo

http://en.wikipedia.org/wiki/Sistine_chapel

http://en.wikipedia.org/wiki/Sekhmet

http://members.westnet.com.au/gary-david-thompson/page11-19.html

http://www.europa.com/~edge/pyramid.html

http://www.pyramidcode.com/

http://www.robertschoch.com/sphinxcontent.html

http://en.wikipedia.org/wiki/Ra

http://en.wikipedia.org/wiki/Great_Sphinx_of_Giza

http://theartofbottledpoetry.wordpress.com/2010/03/08/wine-making-of-ancient-egyptians/

http://en.wikipedia.org/wiki/Prehistoric

http://en.wikipedia.org/wiki/Pottery

http://ancientegyptonline.co.uk/Denderahlightbulb.html

http://en.wikipedia.org/wiki/Baghdad_Battery

http://en.wikipedia.org/wiki/Lascaux

http://www.imdb.com/title/tt0380396/

http://en.wikipedia.org/wiki/Tree_of_life

http://en.wikipedia.org/wiki/Sumer

http://en.wikipedia.org/wiki/Stargate_%28film%29

Thanks to; Gary Hicks, Brian Taylor, Rodrigo Soto, Laird Scranton, Carol Horn, Bob Newton, Anne Tittensor, David McCall, MUFON Australia and anyone else I've missed.

Printed in Great Britain
by Amazon.co.uk, Ltd.,
Marston Gate.